BEYOND CONFLICT

Edited by Timothy Phillips, Mary Albon, Ina Breuer and David Taffel

With a Special Tribute to Nelson Mandela

THE PROJECT ON JUSTICE IN TIMES OF TRANSITION

20 YEARS OF PUTTING EXPERIENCE TO WORK FOR PEACE

DEDICATION

The approach of the Project on Justice in Times of Transition to the seemingly intractable problems of conflict and reconciliation is profoundly simple—to demonstrate through the experience of others that change and coexistance with one's bitter enemies are possible. Oscar Arias, the 1987 Nobel Laureate for Peace, distilled the heart of the Project's mission during his keynote speech at the Project on Justice in Times of Transition conference in Belfast, Northern Ireland, in 1995:

"You have marched, denounced, demanded, divided, slayed, bombed and even starved yourselves to death at times. . . . You say it is difficult to achieve peace here? Yes, perhaps it is. But it was not easy in South Africa. It was not easy in El Salvador. It is not easy in Israel and Palestine. And yet it is happening. And if it can happen there, why not here?"

This book is dedicated to the memory of three extraordinary individuals who showed that peaceful change was possible and, through the courage of their example, shaped history and left a lasting legacy that resonates to this day:

Václav Havel, President, Czech Republic

David Ervine, Leader, Progressive Unionist Party, Northern Ireland

Leonel Gomez, Human Rights Advocate, El Salvador

TABLE OF CONTENTS

A SPECIAL TRIBUTE
TO NELSON MANDELA

At the outset of this book we would like to pay special tribute to one of our distinguished International Advisory Board members, President Nelson Mandela, whose singular leadership, vision and dedication to democracy and reconciliation in South Africa inspired millions around the world. His words at an address he gave at the Oxford Centre for Islamic Studies on July 11, 1997 capture the essence of our work.

By bringing Apartheid to an end—with the support of the whole international community—the people of South Africa have created conditions that are favorable for realizing our vision of a new society based on justice and mutual respect. Non-racialism, non-sexism and democracy. Such a project requires a total transformation of our society with the central objective of addressing the legacy of our divided and oppressive past. . . . This is a project which requires the simultaneous achievement of legitimate government; sustained economic growth in order to bring about socio-economic improvement; and the reconciliation of formerly divided sectors of society.

Being latecomers to freedom and democracy, we have the benefit of the experience of others. Through them, we understand that formal political rights will remain an empty shell and democracy fragile, without real improvement in the lives of people and without an all-inclusive approach that reconciles the beneficiaries of the old order with those who seek improvement from the new. Under the new conditions, in which all are included and equal rights are accorded to all the religions, all the languages and all the cultures of our diverse society, what was once used to divide us and weaken us is becoming a source of unity and strength. . . .

Belief in the possibility of change and renewal is perhaps one of the defining characteristics of politics and of religions. There have been other times when humanity believed that it was poised to enter a new era defined by the achievement of shared ideals. The establishment of the United Nations and the beginning of decolonization was such a time. . . . And can we again call upon the great spiritual values to help inspire humanity to rise to the best potential in itself, and this time truly to achieve those shared ideals for a better world for all its inhabitants? . . . The spirit of Ubuntu—that profound African sense that we are human only through the humanity of other human beings—is not a parochial phenomenon, but has added globally to our common search for a better world . . .

PREFACE

Imagining the Possibility of Change

by Timothy Phillips

Twenty years ago, the Project on Justice in Times of Transition set out to help the new leaders of post-communist Europe figure out how to deal with the painful legacies of their past, which threatened to undermine their emerging democracies. The idea was that they could learn from the experience of leaders in other countries who had successfully guided their own nations through the challenges of moving from dictatorship to democracy or from conflict to peace. The Project started as an experiment, one that was greeted with skepticism even by some of the participants in its first meeting in Salzburg, Austria, in March 1992. Its untested approach was grounded in nothing more than a firm belief in the power of shared human experience that transcends national boundaries. At the time, we didn't realize that we were blazing a trail into a new field, which came to be known as "transitional justice." We never imagined that over the next two decades, the Project would carry out more than 65 initiatives around the world involving hundreds of leaders from more than 50 countries. And we never expected that we would still be at the forefront 20 years on, as we explore the exciting possibilities for conflict resolution at the nexus of science and practice.

I am grateful that my co-founder, Wendy Luers, recognized the potential in the spark of an idea for a conference that I brought to her in November 1991. Wendy had lived and worked in both Latin America and Eastern Europe, so she knew firsthand the risks and perils of life under dictatorship, and she shared my conviction that the new post-communist leaders could learn from the experiences of leaders in Latin America and elsewhere. What we did not know when we convened a group of leaders from these and other regions in Salzburg a few months later was whether the East Europeans would in fact hear what their counterparts had to say. Many insisted that their nation's history and challenges were unique and that there was nothing to be learned from the experience of other countries. But gradually, over the course of several days of discussions and informal conversations over beer and fine food, they began to see parallels and lessons in the experiences of Argentina, Chile, Spain, Uruguay and other countries. The East Europeans returned to their own countries with new perspectives and constructive approaches to developing and instituting their own mechanisms for dealing with the past.

Václav Havel, Czechoslovakia's first democratically elected president after the Velvet Revolution, urged us to continue using the pioneering methodology of "shared experience" that emerged in Salzburg to help the post-communist countries and others grappling with the

9

Founding members of the Project on Justice in Times of Transition (Herman Schwartz, Lloyd Culter, Wendy Luers, Tim Phillips) with President Alfonsín, President Havel and Ruti Teitel, Prague Castle, 1992.

challenges of transition. He encouraged us to formalize our initiative by establishing the Project on Justice in Times of Transition. Soon the Project was working in Central America and South Africa as well as Eastern Europe, and we began to address a much broader range of issues facing countries emerging from dictatorship or violent conflict. Within a few years, the Project was also deeply engaged in Northern Ireland and the Balkans. The Project became known as a trusted, neutral facilitator of shared experience that often leads to productive dialogue within countries and regions emerging from, or still mired in, what had long seemed intractable conflicts. We responded quickly to emerging needs, mobilizing our ever-growing global network of leaders to share their stories and offer advice on navigating the political, legal and moral challenges of transition. The Project's activities continued to expand:

we engaged with leaders in Colombia, the Middle East, Iraq and Sri Lanka. The United Nations asked us to work with senior policymakers to improve their peacebuilding practice. We did work on intelligence reform in Peru and Guatemala. Today our focus is chiefly on Bahrain, Cuba, Kosovo and Turkey.

It is not uncommon to see one-time bitter enemies sitting side by side on Project panels, including historic figures like Poland's former communist leader, General Wojciech Jaruzelski, who imposed martial law, and the former dissident and Solidarity activist Adam Michnik; or Joaquín Villalobos, who had been a guerilla leader in El Salvador, and Alfredo Cristiani, the country's former president; or Martin McGuinness, the former IRA commander who now serves as Northern Ireland's Deputy First Minister, and the Reverend Ian Paisley, founder of the

Democratic Unionist Party and former First Minister of Northern Ireland. The impact of this kind of juxtaposition is intensely powerful and deeply jarring to those who could never imagine that former adversaries and even once deadly foes could sit together, work together and slowly grow to respect and trust each other. Many of the leaders we have worked with have told me they feel a moral obligation to share their profound experience of transformation with their counterparts in other countries struggling with change. This has turned out to be one of the most valuable outcomes of the Project's work over the years.

The Project's focus on the commonalities of human experience has also led us into the realm of neuroscience. Our work has demonstrated not only that people can learn from the experience of others, but also that they can change. Even in deeply divided societies, people can move away from a zero-sum outlook to one in which compromise is not a sign of weakness or humiliation, but is in fact a sign of courage and strength that leads to a common good. Today the Project is working with neuroscientists to better understand the mental and biological processes that can prompt this kind of change.

If there is one central lesson I have learned from my work with the Project on Justice in Times of Transition, it is that transformative change, while difficult to attain, is possible. Yet efforts to achieve peace are often hindered by a self-defeating conviction that change is impossible. But just think what could be achieved if this outlook were abandoned. Imagine the Israeli Prime Minister sitting down with the leader of Hezbollah to negotiate a peace agreement—that's impossible, you think—there's too deep a history of hatred, distrust and killing between their communities. But if they took this bold step, they could lay the groundwork for an enduring peace that would completely change the Middle East and beyond.

The challenge we face is to imagine the unimaginable, to find creative solutions to problems that seem immune to resolution—and to prove that they are not.

TOP: Yitzhak Rabin and Yasser Arafat after the signing of the Oslo Peace Accords in 1993. MIDDLE: Adam Michnik and General Jaruzelski at Project initiative, "Reflections on Transition," Nicaragua, 1994. BOTTOM: Ian Paisley and Gerry Adams at Stormont after the signing of the power sharing agreement in 2007.

The Power of Shared Experience

by Timothy Phillips

Considerable human, political and financial resources have been devoted to resolving conflict and ending dictatorship over the past century, yet war, violence and repression remain a significant part of daily global experience. Even in places where peace treaties have been signed or dictatorships have fallen, achieving sustainable peace and building effective democracy have proven difficult. This is especially true in deeply divided societies like Israel and Palestine, Bosnia & Herzegovina and Sri Lanka, where competing narratives and a range of regional and global dynamics keep citizens under constant threat of renewed violence and repression.

A key question facing us as we look to current challenges in the Middle East and North Africa and to emerging global threats is: *What are we missing?* To be better prepared to confront these challenges, we need to understand the mechanisms of human behavior that drive individuals and groups into and away from repression and violent conflict. This is what the Project on Justice in Times of Transition seeks to do. By focusing on the personal transformations demanded of individual leaders, the Project helps them to understand the fundamental changes in perceptions and actions that will be required of them if they and their countries are to achieve genuine change. Emphasizing the human dimension of conflict transformation, the Project has helped to clear the path for progress in peace talks, democratic transitions and national reconciliation in countries around the globe.

FINDING COMMON TRUTHS THROUGH SHARED EXPERIENCE

In 1992, the Project on Justice in Times of Transition developed a simple yet powerful methodology of *shared experience* to assist leaders in divided societies struggling with conflict, reconciliation and societal change. It is grounded in two core principles: that *people can learn from each other*, and that *people can change*. This methodology stems from the insight that on a biological, emotional and psychological level, humans have many of the same response mechanisms to the formative experiences of their lives. While it is true that every country has its own unique national experience and history, how people around the world respond to the terrifying, humiliating and dehumanizing experience of life under dictatorship or during civil war is fundamentally the same. What the Project founders

Participants at the 1992 founding meeting of the Project on Justice in Times of Transition in Salzburg, Austria.

understood intuitively, and humbly, was that people in these situations struggle as individuals on a deeply personal and psychological level with the burdens of violence, fear and repression. But we also understood that it was possible to move beyond these terrible experiences, and that learning about the experiences of others who had done so could help speed the process of both internal and societal change.

By bringing leaders from countries around the world to share their experiences in addressing conflict or repression with their counterparts in a country in the midst of grappling with similar challenges, the Project has helped build trust between once bitter enemies in what were seemingly intractable conflicts, and has given leaders the courage to introduce changes key to generating peace.

In countries transitioning from dictatorship or long-standing conflict, individuals commonly develop a very insular view of their own reality: they believe no one else has suffered the way they have suffered, that no one else can understand the horrible experience they have endured, and that differences in culture, history, language and geography are too great to allow for any cross-cultural learning. Feelings of victimhood are extremely powerful and can stymie any attempt to engage with the enemy or pursue reconciliation until this suffering is acknowledged and validated. Often both sides in a conflict feel victimized, which makes it even more difficult to think about a shared future and engage in meaningful dialogue.

People in societies emerging from conflict or repression also tend to be reluctant to listen to or

"For the first time I recognized that although
we were political opponents, although in
the conflict we were enemies, we also had suffered loss,
each of us. We needed to reach beyond the
sense of being opponents and enemies to recognize
that on both sides there had been suffering,
on both sides there had been loss."

—Jeffrey Donaldson, Northern Ireland Politician, DUP,
Member of Parliament in the United Kingdom

respect the views of outsiders, developing a "deafness" to others as a self-defense mechanism that can be difficult to penetrate. This inward-looking perspective often stems in part from the vertically divided social structure of many countries where there is little or no interaction across class, ethnic, religious or political allegiances. It also arises in countries where bonds of trust have been destroyed by years (or even decades) of violence and repression, leaving people unprepared to respect or value the views or experience of others, whether they be opponents or outsiders.

Another dynamic seen in societies long divided by conflict or political repression is that any hint of change, compromise or accommodation with your "enemy" is seen as a betrayal of your own community, of your family, ancestors and neighbors. Decades of violence and polarization harden attitudes, creating a political and psychological environment that makes it difficult for leaders as well as ordinary people to consider changing their views or "talking peace" with their sworn enemies. Often the leaders of peace negotiations or a national transition process that the

Project seeks to help do not recognize that they have a problem.

Understanding and respecting these realities, the Project structures its programs to carefully yet powerfully show people who are not psychologically prepared to listen to outsiders that "others" have something valuable to offer. We do this by drawing on the Project's globe-spanning network of widely respected, compassionate and articulate national leaders to serve

Co-founders Wendy Luers and Tim Phillips with Václav Havel, 2007.

> "We learn that the impossible is possible,
> the ways of transformation are infinite,
> the new difficulties are enormous, and yet life is
> emphatically better at the end."
>
> —Albie Sachs, former Justice of South African Constitutional Court,
> former African National Congress activist

as panelists and speakers in our programs. These are people who have led peace processes, managed negotiations, struggled with ceasefires and breakdowns in talks, sought to build trust and accountability and promoted reconciliation. What these leaders bring to the table are their own stories. They often share deeply personal experiences, such as how they felt the first time they sat down across the negotiating table from their sworn enemies, or the moment that prompted them to realize that violence was not helping their cause but only hurting people.

These narratives are not unique to an individual situation or country; they address universal challenges leaders face in conflict situations that are fundamental to finding a way out—both for the individual and society. They also represent a set of emotions and psychological shifts that need to be better understood by conflict practitioners and diplomats working to end conflicts and achieve peaceful transitions. By sharing their personal stories, these leaders challenge their audience to look at their own problems in a new light, to recognize that change is possible and to think about what they can and must do to make change happen. The leaders in our network know the right questions to ask to actively engage their audience in this intense process of personal reflection and transformation, and

to help them identify, prepare for and address the challenges they face.

Often the intensity of our speakers' own past suffering cuts through the inability of audience members to listen. Hearing the powerful story of another's anguish is a sad but necessary element to a breakthrough in perception and possibility. In essence, what our participants discover is that, "if this person could move beyond such pain and anger, then I can too." Two powerful examples of such moments follow.

IMPRISONED BY MYTHOLOGY

David Ervine, a former member of a Protestant Loyalist paramilitary organization in Northern Ireland who spent nearly a decade in prison for resistance activities and later served as a leader of the Progressive Unionist Party, provided a forceful example of personal transformation. When David emerged from prison, he became one of the leading Loyalist political voices calling for peace and negotiations to end more than 30 years of civil war.

In 2006, shortly before his untimely death from a heart attack, David shared his life story with senior leaders of the ELN guerilla movement in Colombia in a Project initiative designed to reengage the ELN in peace talks and initiate a ceasefire agreement with the Colombian government. David told the Colombians that he joined the paramilitary Ulster Volunteer Force (UVF) when he was 17 years old on the day he learned that another Protestant boy, of the same age and with the same last name, had been killed by a bomb planted by the Irish Republican Army (IRA). Stunned and traumatized by the event, which took on added resonance for him because of the victim's similar name and age, David joined the UVF, convinced that the only defense against such random violence was a good offense, and that he could no longer stand by but must defend his community, his identity and way of life, all of which he saw as under threat. He told the Colombian guerillas that in the beginning, he believed he was killing "others" to live, but gradually, as the violence and dehumanizing impact of the conflict took over, he realized he was living to kill.

David emphasized that all liberation and paramilitary groups develop their own mythology and justification for the acts of violence and terrorism they commit, but that mythology imprisons them in a mindset that can be extraordinarily difficult to

Ricardo Castaneda, former Salvadoran ambassador to the UN; James LeMoyne, former NYT Bureau Chief in El Salvador; and Joaquín Villalobos, former FMLN guerilla leader, at 1996 Project initiative, "Workshop on Reconciliation for Bosnia" held in London.

transcend. David's audience was transfixed by his story. The powerful insights he shared connected him to the ELN commanders at a deeply personal level, and they immediately recognized a similar dynamic in their own situation. As a result, they were willing to listen to his advice about what to consider as the ELN negotiated a ceasefire with the Colombian government and what sort of transformations to prepare for—both personally and as a guerilla movement transforming itself into a legitimate political party.

A HISTORY OF VIOLENCE—AND SUFFERING

Another important moment occurred in London in 1995 during a Project meeting that brought together leaders of the Muslim, Serb and Croat communities in Bosnia & Herzegovina to foster reconciliation after the signing of the Dayton Peace Accords. The event highlighted examples of reconciliation in El Salvador, Northern Ireland, the Middle East and Central and Eastern Europe. The opening session of the conference fell flat; the Bosnians tuned out the presentations and vented about their own conflict and suffering, emphasizing that no one could appreciate or understand the trauma they had just passed through. This is a common initial reaction at many Project events, but this time there was real concern that the Bosnians might never really listen to what the international speakers had to say. But then James LeMoyne, moderator of the panel on reconciliation in El Salvador who had been the New York Times bureau chief in El Salvador during the worst of the conflict, took a dramatic new tack in introducing the Salvadoran panelists.

First LeMoyne introduced Ricardo Castaneda, the former Salvadoran ambassador to the United Nations and a key figure in the peace negotiations, by describing

Protestors in Tahir Square, Egypt in January 2011.

how on one occasion when he went to the ambassador's home in San Salvador to attend a dinner for foreign diplomats, he found the bodies of several campesino labor leaders who had been tortured, eviscerated and dumped in front of the ambassador's house to intimidate him from participating in the peace talks. The killers of the campesinos were not from the guerilla movement but from the right-wing death squads who were hostile to the peace process. After hearing this introduction, the Bosnians stopped talking with each other and started to listen to James. He then introduced Joaquín Villalobos, former senior commander of the FMLN guerilla movement in El Salvador and one of the most brilliant and brutal guerilla leaders in Latin American history, who ultimately abandoned violence in favor of participating in a negotiated political process and led the FMLN toward peace. James told the horrific story of how Villalobos's girlfriend, who was also a guerilla fighter, had been captured by the Salvadoran army, tortured and dismembered into more than 70 pieces which were left in a bag for Villalobos to find. As horrendous as these introductions were, they cut through the "differences" between El Salvador and Bosnia, commanding the attention of the Bosnians, who thereafter listened intently to the story of how the two sides reached peace in El Salvador by working together to build trust and foster national reconciliation in the aftermath of a brutally violent civil war.

These and other examples of personal stories shared by leaders at Project initiatives are so profound and so startling that they often inspire the target audience to reconsider their own positions or ideas, helping them not only to recognize that change is possible, but emboldening them to take the first steps toward compromise. Once it was inconceivable that certain conflicts could be ended, so to hear from the people who succeeded in ending them is one of the most powerful tools we have for showing leaders of countries emerging from conflict that they too can bring positive change to their homelands. Our international speakers demonstrate by their own example that although change requires leadership—and courage—everyone has the capacity to exercise such leadership, and indeed, it is the duty of leaders in societies riven by conflict or repression to strive for change that can bring about peace, stability and national reconciliation.

THE PSYCHOLOGY OF CHANGE

Achieving fundamental change, whether at the deeply personal or national political level, is a profoundly difficult and painful process that can take years to happen, if it does at all. It requires not only leadership but courage, and a willingness to take both personal and political risks. The extraordinary network of current and former leaders who work with the Project on Justice in Times of Transition have all undergone personal transformations that helped them to push toward peace and stability in their own countries, and they understand both the external and internal challenges that leaders must overcome and the risks they must take to achieve transformational change.

They intuitively understand, empathize with and want to support leaders currently struggling with the thorny challenges of transition from repression or conflict to peace. They work with the Project to help these leaders achieve the difficult but necessary processes of personal and national transformation that will enable them to guide their countries to peace.

This book highlights some of the most important overarching themes that the Project on Justice in Times of Transition addresses in its work from the perspective of six prominent leaders in our network. These themes include:

- **Confronting Dictatorship**
- **Recognizing the Need for Change**
- **Changing Entrenched Mindsets**
- **Building Trust Among Enemies**
- **Compromising with the Other Side**
- **Confronting the Past and Forging a Shared Vision for the Future**

The six remarkable leaders, who come from the Czech Republic, South Africa, Guatemala, Northern Ireland, Israel and Chile, have personally grappled with these issues, in some cases putting their lives on the line as they strove to find ways to heal their divided nations. They have also worked with the Project on Justice in Times of Transition to help other leaders around the globe tackle these challenges. In the following pages, they reflect on how they overcame these obstacles in their own contexts, and how their thinking has evolved over the 20 years that they have been involved with the Project. Their stories, which are representative of the work of the Project on Justice in Times of Transition, vividly illustrate the human dimension of change that is essential to achieving sustainable peace after war and repression.

CZECHOSLOVAKIA

1918 The Republic of Czechoslovakia is created post WWI as part of the Treaty of Versailles.

1938-45 The German occupation of Czechoslovakia begins when Nazi forces invade Czechoslovakia, taking over Bohemia and establishing a protectorate over Slovakia.

1945 Soviet troops enter Prague in the Prague Offensive, resulting in the Soviet liberation of Prague from German forces.

1948 Communist rule begins with a coup d'etat. Free elections are abolished.

1968 The Prague Spring begins with the Czechoslovak Communist Party leader Alexander Dubcek's attempt to liberalize Czechoslovakia by introducing free speech and assembly. The Prague Spring ends with the Warsaw Pact's invasion of Prague. Most of Dubcek's liberalizing reforms are reversed.

1977 Dissident Czechoslovakian intellectuals write Charter 77, a declaration and petition which demands that the Communist government recognize basic human rights.

1989 The Velvet Revolution brings the fall of the Communist Party through peaceful demonstrations and leaders of Charter 77, including Jan Urban, play an important role in establishing new democratic institutions.

1993 Czechoslovakia officially completes the "Velvet Divorce," resulting in the creation of the Czech Republic and Slovakia.

JAN URBAN

Confronting Dictatorship

As a young boy in communist Czechoslovakia, Jan Urban presented flowers to Nikita Khrushchev, Ho Chi Minh, Che Guevara and other dignitaries from socialist countries around the world when they visited Prague. Urban and his schoolmates were trained to believe that "we were part of the communist vanguard—the future was ours." Yet by the time he was a teenager, this privileged son of committed communists had turned against the regime, refusing to conform to the oppressive rules it imposed on every aspect of daily life. He endured two decades of intimidation and harassment at the hands of the secret police, but he never gave up hope that one day things would change, though he never quite believed that he would see that day himself. "I just wanted to do as much damage to the communist regime as possible," Urban says, "but I did not personally believe that I would see the end of it, until the very end."

Defying dictatorship takes constant courage and conviction, and a willingness to keep struggling despite persecution and what might seem impossible odds. The life of a political dissident is difficult, dangerous and often lonely, and it scars even those who ultimately succeed in bringing change. And change itself poses new challenges for dissidents, ones which, Urban readily admits, they may be unprepared to confront.

THE MAKING OF A DISSIDENT

In considering the factors that turned him into a fierce opponent of communism, Urban says that "being a rebel and being willing to go against dictatorship was sort of a family tradition." Although his parents were both "true communist enthusiasts and believers," they were among the first to recognize the dark side of Czechoslovakia's Stalinist regime. His father was expelled from the Communist Party Central Committee in the early 1960s, but because he had spent six years fighting the Nazis in the communist resistance, he was spared prison; instead, he was appointed ambassador to Finland.

Leading Czechoslovak and Polish dissidents, including Jan Urban, Václav Havel, Jacek Kuroń, Adam Michnik and Zbigniew Bujak, meeting secretly on the border in 1988.

Life in the West opened Urban's eyes to a new reality that contradicted everything he had been taught. In the summer of 1968, when he was 16 years old, Urban visited London—"my first exposure to real imperialists," he recalls. "When you grow up as a subject of ideological indoctrination and then you realize that people in the West are absolutely normal people, with not only two legs and two hands, but normal kinds of reasons for laughter and for trying to differentiate between good and bad," Urban says, you can no longer accept what you have been taught. He also credits "rock and roll, blue jeans, Bob Dylan, Joan Baez and all this cultural revolt of the 1960s" and its emphasis on freedom and self-expression for opening his eyes to new ways of looking at the world and the system in which he had grown up.

But the decisive factor in his transformation from complacent citizen into outspoken dissident was Czechoslovakia's brief flowering of political and cultural liberalization in 1968 known as the Prague Spring and the Soviet-led invasion that forcibly quashed it. "When you see Soviet tanks and soldiers shooting madly around your city," says Urban, "that sends a message that cannot be overlooked." He realized that the time had come "not for polishing the surface of the communist system, but for changing it."

"After '68 it was simple," Urban says. "Once you start getting into conflicts with the secret police or the Communist Party, that is a sort of training, and if you don't break down or are not broken in interrogations, then you are lucky and you end as a dissident. And that's what happened to me."

PERSONALIZING OPPRESSION

The crushing of the Prague Spring ushered in "a very dark two decades," Urban says. The new, hard-line government introduced a policy of "normalization," which reversed the reforms of the Prague Spring, reinstated censorship and deployed the blunt tools of repression to enforce popular compliance with the regime. "The state apparatus succeeded beyond any imagination in making oppression personal," Urban asserts. Anything not explicitly approved by the regime could be interpreted as a sign of protest.

"Everything was political," Urban recalls. "Whatever you did, the people you met on the streets, whom you called, the books you had at home—everything had a political connotation, undertone, meaning." It was a system of social control based on humiliation and enforced by fear. The safest approach was passive collaboration—to express no opinions, to keep your head down and avoid making eye contact with anyone in the street. People tried to be invisible, unnoticed—"and that turned us into a people without personality," Urban says. Passivity on this mass scale "proved to be the most difficult thing to change after 1989." In subsequent years, Urban has seen similar behavior in other repressive societies.

"No one except the dissidents was willing or able to raise their voice against the communists," Urban notes. Dissidents wrote and shared underground newspapers, books and plays, created unauthorized art and talked about forbidden concepts like democracy and human rights. But they were only a small island of independent thought in a vast gray sea of fear and conformity.

"There were so few dissidents in Czechoslovakia that the prospect of changing the regime seemed impossible," Urban says, "so it was a more personal revolt based on moral grounds than a political resistance." In contrast to neighboring Poland, where the unofficial Solidarity trade union had 10 million members and the dissident movement established hundreds of underground newspapers, publishing houses and a radio station, Czechoslovakia had only a small community of active dissidents who were, according to Urban, "unable to reach out to society until very, very late." In his view, this was a significant failing. "We somehow did not realize that even in the darkest days, we needed to reach out to the rest of society, we needed to be more active, to test the limits more actively than we did."

CRACKDOWN ON DISSENTERS

The level of repression increased in 1977, when a group of dissidents signed a statement criticizing Czechoslovakia's human rights record and attempted to present it to the government. Co-written by the playwright Václav Havel and several others, this unsanctioned petition known as Charter 77 was quickly confiscated. But the text was published in leading Western newspapers, broadcast into Czechoslovakia by Radio Free Europe and other banned stations, and self-published *samizdat* copies circulated throughout the country. Because he refused to sign a statement condemning Charter 77, Urban lost his job as a high school teacher.

Czechoslovakia's state security police, the StB, kept dissidents like Urban under close surveillance, tapping their phones, bugging their apartments, following them and compiling detailed records of their activities and interactions with other people. The StB was aided and abetted by a vast network of informal spies and collaborators who reported on their neighbors, colleagues and sometimes even friends and family. As punishment for challenging communist authority, dissidents were arrested, interrogated and imprisoned. They were prohibited from practicing their professions, and their children's education was restricted. Some were coerced into collaborating with the StB.

Despite beatings, imprisonment and the harassment of his family, Urban continued to resist. He worked as a manual laborer to support his family, but he also wrote for an underground newspaper and reported for Radio Free Europe and the BBC. In 1988, he co-founded the Eastern European Information Agency, a network of dissident journalists in Czechoslovakia, Poland, Hungary and the USSR. Working as a journalist was empowering. "You escape the sense of being a victim and always being defeated," he says. "Getting your information out is also a way to hit back."

Urban refused to let the regime blackmail him through his children or his parents. But when his father died of a heart attack in 1988 after three days of interrogation, "I lived on pure hatred," Urban admits. "I planned, I prepared, I was willing to kill." He only stopped himself when he realized that was exactly what the regime wanted.

WOULD CHANGE REALLY COME?

"When you run for 20 years, when you fight for 20 years, you know nothing else," says Urban. But by 1989, things were starting to change in neighboring countries. In the Soviet Union, Mikhail Gorbachev was encouraging "New Thinking" and making peaceful overtures toward the West. In Poland, Solidarity was emboldened, no longer afraid that Soviet military intervention would crush it like it had the Prague Spring. By the summer of 1989, Poland had negotiated a transition and elected a new, democratic government.

Hungary had opened its borders to the West and thousands of East Germans were pouring through them en route to West Germany. But in Czechoslovakia, the repression did not let up. "In the summer of '89, I received a coffin with my name on it as a threat from the secret police," Urban recalls. "I was getting death threats on the phone." Despite what was happening elsewhere, he did not believe that change would come to his country.

Urban recounts a visit that summer from his friend, the Polish dissident Adam Michnik, and several other members of Solidarity who had recently been elected to parliament. Just one year earlier, they had met at clandestine gatherings of Polish and Czechoslovak dissidents in the mountains on their shared border. Now they were walking openly together in the streets of Prague. On a nighttime stroll through the city, Urban remembers feeling paranoid, aware that the secret police were keeping a close eye on them. "Adam was laughing like mad, pointing at the red neon stars and all these neon communist slogans on the buildings in the center of the town," Urban recalls. "He said, 'Do you want to bet that a year from now there won't be one red star here?' I tried to calm him down and said that this was not Poland, this was different. But he said, 'Don't you get it? It's over.'" Urban is still a bit astonished at his own blindness. "Because Adam was a beloved friend, I didn't want to argue," he continues. "I thought that he didn't get the difference between Poland and Czechoslovakia. But he was right. In four months' time, we were forming the government without even seeing it coming."

The speed of the regime's collapse came as a surprise to Urban and many others. "I remember watching the fall of the Berlin Wall"—in November 1989—"and still we were not sure that something similar would happen in Czechoslovakia," he recalls. Yet the following month it did.

THE WHITE TIGER LEAVES ITS CAGE

In November 1989, the whole world watched in wonder and delight as Czech and Slovak students, actors and writers took to the streets and stages of Prague and Bratislava to demand an end to communist repression. In just a few weeks, the Velvet Revolution brought about the peaceful demise of Czechoslovakia's iron-fisted communist regime.

The Velvet Revolution was an improvisation. Responding to a wave of student protests in mid-November, dissidents and intellectuals quickly created independent organizations—Civic Forum, led by Václav Havel, in the Czech Republic, and Public Against Violence in Slovakia—that successfully called for a general strike. Within a matter of days, the communist leadership bowed to the popular will and resigned. Havel, Urban and other dissidents were suddenly catapulted into positions of authority. In December 1989, Havel was elected president, and a little later Urban took over as head of Civic Forum.

Yet Urban is critical of the dissidents. When the regime collapsed and they had to take power, "we were totally unprepared," he says. In his view, "the inability to prepare ourselves for the change and for the coming crisis was the most dramatic intellectual failure of modern Czech history."

Jan Urban at Project initiative, "The Future of Peace in Northern Ireland," Belfast, 1995.

"When you spend most of your time as a victim,
or believing yourself to be a victim, there's
no responsibility attached. All of your life is decided
outside of you, and whatever you do is right simply
because you are a victim and you suffer. So
you believe that you are above the law, above morality,
above everything simply because you are a victim.
Consequently, people who have experienced long
trauma or long conflict are very passive."

Czechoslovak society was not ready for change either. Urban uses the analogy of a white tiger born in a zoo. "All of a sudden somebody opens the cage and tells you to get out and be on your own. As a white tiger, you stand no chance in the jungle, but you still want to survive. So you have to change yourself completely." What this requires is "a sort of mental rehabilitation," which is an incredibly difficult and painful process, "a form of post-traumatic stress disorder played out at the national level."

"When you spend most of your time as a victim, or believing yourself to be a victim, there's no responsibility attached," says Urban. "All of your life is decided outside of you, and whatever you do is right simply because you are a victim and you suffer. So you believe that you are above the law, above morality, above everything simply because you are a victim." Consequently, "people who

have experienced long trauma or long conflict are very passive and this is difficult to change." Any change creates fear "because experience tells them that whatever changed was for the worse." The status quo seems safer than venturing into the unknown. Citizens don't want to make decisions, and in fact they do not know how.

THE NECESSITY OF COMPROMISE

The self-righteousness of the victim mentality also leads to an inability to compromise. "This was the malaise that Czechoslovak dissidents had," says Urban. "Instead of looking for a sufficient consensus, we looked for an ideal solution. The end result was the breakup of Czechoslovakia."

"The Polish dissidents were able to compromise and show great statesmanship," he says. "But we did not

"What I call the third element is helpful. Somebody from the outside, somebody who can in a convincing way convey the message that 'you are not unique.'"

know how to make compromise. And we did not have the will to make compromise." This, he insists, "is the main reason why the absolute majority of our dissidents, including Václav Havel, lost in politics."

It was also the reason that Urban left politics. "I understood in a very painful manner that I am not able to make compromise," he admits. "If you cannot make compromise you should not get into politics." In June 1990, the day after the communists were roundly defeated in parliamentary elections, Urban resigned his post as head of Civic Forum and returned to journalism.

If you are unable to compromise, you may end up achieving nothing. "I have learned that in all conflicts we should look for people who are able to accept the need to look for the lowest common denominator," Urban says. He cites an example from Iraq, where he took part in reconciliation efforts after Saddam Hussein's regime was overthrown. "Everybody wanted to preserve cultural monuments. All of a sudden people who wouldn't talk to each other found the lowest common denominator visible and possible. And it worked." The Iraqis were able to work together toward a common goal, which helped in a small way to begin to reduce tensions and enabled additional steps toward reconciliation.

This is also where Urban sees a role for outsiders. "What I call the third element is helpful," he says. "Somebody from

the outside, somebody who can in a convincing way convey the message that 'you are not unique.'" The most effective are those who have dealt with similar challenges and can share their own experiences. "I started to understand Czechoslovakia and our problems exactly because I was able to see similarities to the problems of El Salvador and other countries," Urban says. His involvement with the Project on Justice in Times of Transition showed him approaches to reconciliation that other countries had taken.

Urban recalls his astonishment at learning about the truth commission concept. "It was so non-black-and-white. It really changed my life completely." He points out that of all the post-communist countries in Central and Eastern Europe and the former Soviet Union, "not one of them had the courage to use the truth commission concept. Why? Because we are poisoned by this absolutely black-and-white, dictatorial communist ideology that is still inside us. We do not understand that the country needs something else than we do, that there's no one eternal truth." There is also an element of cowardice. "We want symbolic punishment but not the truth. We don't want to be revealed as perpetrators or collaborators."

In his country, "it will take generations for people to get back to normalcy," Urban says. The key will come from "learning to make compromises and to put national interests above your own."

SOUTH AFRICA

1948 Official beginning of Apartheid – a series of 317 laws that institutionalized racial segregation.

1964 Nelson Mandela imprisoned for life.

1977 UN imposes an arms and oil embargo and creates a Security Council sanctions committee in Dec.

1979 Roelf Meyer elected as a Member of Parliament for the ruling National Party.

1984–1989 Increasing sanctions against South Africa, solidification of the movement in the United States, growing support for divestment around the world.

1986 Roelf Meyer appointed Deputy Minister of Law and Order.

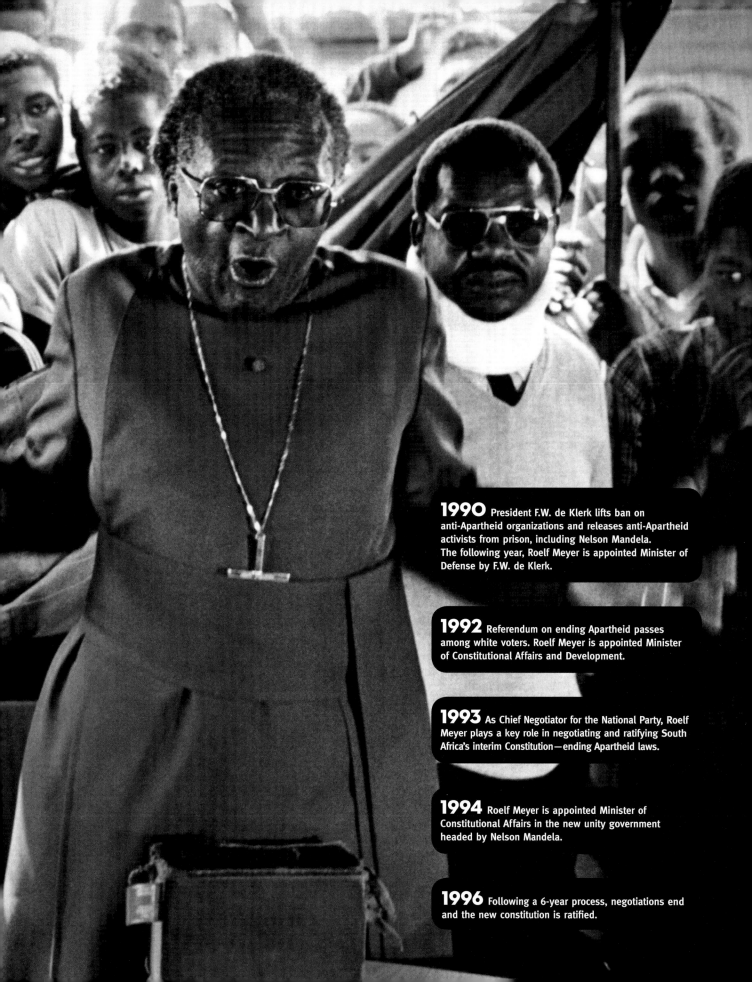

1990 President F.W. de Klerk lifts ban on anti-Apartheid organizations and releases anti-Apartheid activists from prison, including Nelson Mandela. The following year, Roelf Meyer is appointed Minister of Defense by F.W. de Klerk.

1992 Referendum on ending Apartheid passes among white voters. Roelf Meyer is appointed Minister of Constitutional Affairs and Development.

1993 As Chief Negotiator for the National Party, Roelf Meyer plays a key role in negotiating and ratifying South Africa's interim Constitution—ending Apartheid laws.

1994 Roelf Meyer is appointed Minister of Constitutional Affairs in the new unity government headed by Nelson Mandela.

1996 Following a 6-year process, negotiations end and the new constitution is ratified.

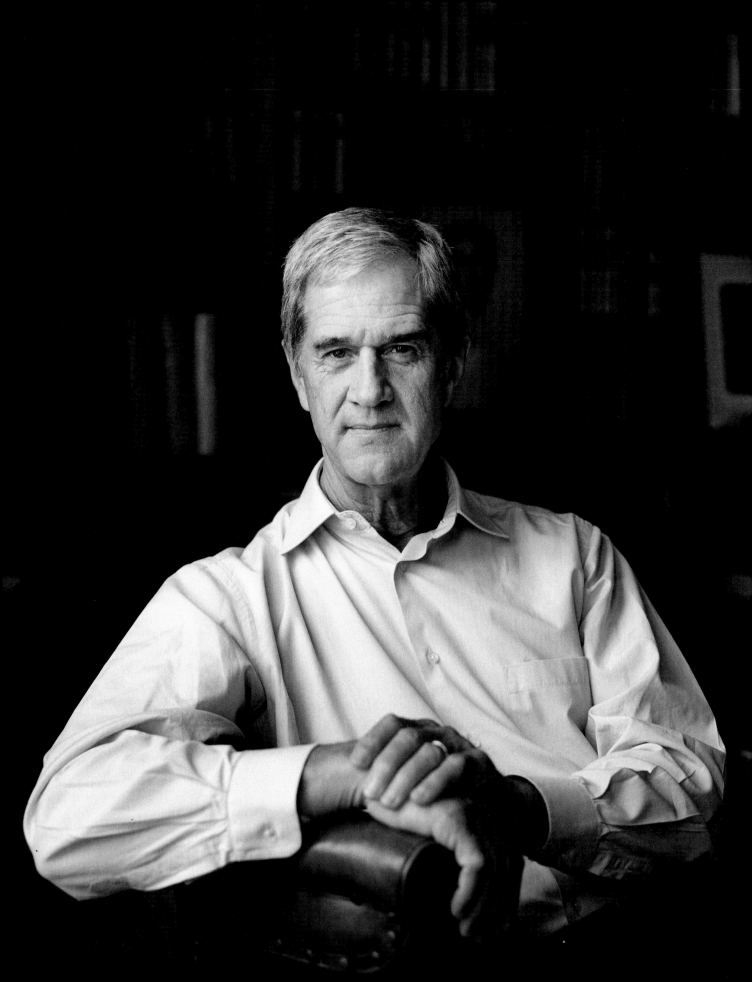

ROELF MEYER

Recognizing the Need for Change

ew people expected that Apartheid, the system of racial segregation and white supremacy enforced by South Africa's National Party from 1948 to 1994, would end peacefully. Perhaps even fewer thought that one of the people who would play an instrumental role in its dismantlement would be a privileged member of Afrikaner society who would have likely become president of South Africa had Apartheid not ended. Roelf Meyer, who started out as a contented beneficiary of Apartheid, eventually became one of the key people who convinced President F. W. de Klerk to release Nelson Mandela from prison and then led the negotiating team of the white-minority government in the talks to end Apartheid. Meyer's personal transformation echoes his nation's path of transition, from one entrenched in centuries-old notions of racial superiority to one that realized the need to strive for equality for all.

APARTHEID'S PRIVILEGED SON

Meyer grew up with advantages and opportunities that his black compatriots could never have imagined or accessed. "When I started to work professionally, times were good for me and my generation," he says. But as a young lawyer grappling with his personal sense of fairness and justice, Meyer was confronted with the reality that blacks and other non-white South Africans had no constitutional rights; seeing that basic denial of dignity enshrined in national laws rocked his value system. He recalls speaking with a former farmhand who explained how he had come to join the insurgent movement. The young man recounted riding in the back of a white farmer's pickup truck when he was a child, along with the farmer's dog. When it began to rain, the farmer brought the dog into the cab to stay dry and left the boy in the open back to get drenched in the downpour. This simple yet profound act of humiliation and insensitivity to another human being, particularly a young child, stunned Meyer. Repeated exposure to such appalling examples of dehumanization and blatant racism and inequality gradually began to eat away at Meyer, pushing him toward the conviction that the system of Apartheid must end and that change must come.

While serving as Vice Minister of Police during a national state of emergency, Meyer was tasked by President P. W. Botha to learn why blacks were rioting. He spent 18 months visiting black townships to gain an understanding of the unrest and what might stop it. Few whites, let alone government officials, ventured into the townships, so it was an eye-opening experience for Meyer to see for himself the harsh reality of black life in South Africa. He began to understand that although he was an elected representative to Parliament, he in no way represented the people of South Africa, but only a tiny white minority whose advantages and privileges he could no longer morally support. During further travels around the country, Meyer realized that the National Party's evolving thinking about negotiating with moderates in the African National Congress (ANC) would not work. If progress were to be made, it would have to deal with the the party's militant wing and its leader, Nelson Mandela.

DAMN LONG BEFORE THE LIGHT

Intellectually, Meyer had come to understand the pragmatic need for drastic social and political change, but it took far longer to feel this need at an emotional and political level. "One might argue it was damn long before I saw the light, but there it was," Meyer says. In all, it took him 14 years to complete his personal transformation. By 1989, he had left behind the old paradigm of white supremacy and black inferiority that had reigned since 1652. "I was able to speak on the other side. I was within

Roelf Meyer and Cyril Ramaphosa observing South African leaders Mangosuthu Buthelezi, F.W. de Klerk and Nelson Mandela after the signing of the agreement to end Apartheid, 1994.

Gerry Adams, President of Sinn Fein, and Roelf Meyer at 1995 Project conference, "The Future of Peace in Northern Ireland" held in Belfast.

international pressure on South Africa; economic sanctions and other punitive measures enacted by the international community; the growing effectiveness of the ANC, which essentially made part of the country ungovernable and led to a years-long state of emergency; and the internal recognition by white South Africans that "change had to come, because the country was bleeding itself to bits" and the existing course would inevitably lead to full-scale civil war.

RECOGNIZING THE NEED FOR CHANGE

When the process of dismantling Apartheid and creating a genuine democracy officially began in 1990, the mindset of most white South Africans had not yet shifted, and especially not among members of the National Party. Despite starting talks and moving forward with negotiations, the National Party was still operating under the same old paradigm of trying to retain as much power for the white minority as possible. Meyer recollects a constitutional proposal for a rotating presidency introduced by the de Klerk government: "It was for one reason only: to exercise a veto by the minority." Until 1992, when the talks broke down, the National Party only grasped the need for change at an intellectual or pragmatic level. "The mind informs the pragmatic shift because it's a calculated change. You can see that factors are against it, there's too much pressure. You have to start change, that's an intellectual innovation," Meyer explains. However, "if you don't buy into that change and accept the consequences, and work towards a different outcome, then it sticks to a pragmatic shift."

The 1992 breakdown "forced us as a government to go back to the drawing board and say to ourselves, 'What now?'" Meyer says. "'What is it that we want from a future Constitution in South Africa?'" Meyer pinpoints that moment as the paradigm shift: it dawned

the new paradigm then, realizing that South Africa's future could only be based on equality for all, in a democratic environment." Meyer not only understood the need for change, he embraced it.

"I have great respect for Roelf," says the South African human rights activist Albie Sachs, who was appointed as a justice of the Constitutional Court by Nelson Mandela. "His personal journey and his continuing commitment constitute a great story in itself, but, as important, keep one's optimism alive for our country and the world." The course of Meyer's personal transformation, from a pragmatic shift in his thinking to a much deeper, more personal paradigm shift, helps explain South Africa's story. It also took a long time for the National Party leadership to recognize the need for change, and when it finally did, in the late 1980s, this recognition was purely pragmatic. As Meyer tells it, "The writing was on the wall. We had to make changes because of a pragmatic realization in President de Klerk's mind and those around him that it had to happen." Meyer often stresses that change is slow and does not come by itself, but is strengthened and enhanced by other dynamics. In South Africa's case, he credits four factors: increasing

TOP: Hashim Thaci, Prime Minister of Kosovo—then leader of PDK Opposition Party—and Roelf Meyer at 2003 Project initiative, "Crafting Strategies for Negotiation." BOTTOM: Mohammad Bhabha, Ben Harburg and Roelf Meyer meeting with deputy foreign minister during 2011 Project visit to Bahrain.

on the National Party government that "this notion of reserved rights, of group rights, of minority protection in the South African environment won't work. And we have to intervene to make one of equality for all." In his view, the breakdown "was the best thing that could have happened because it forced us to go to the next level. And I'm absolutely convinced that if we didn't make the paradigm shift, it would not have been sustainable."

Sometimes it takes a breakdown to move forward. It gives both sides the opportunity to assess their priorities and recommit to finding a solution. "If you want to find a real settlement, you must expect breakdowns," Meyer says. "You also accept the willingness to resume after some difficult breakdowns."

RECOGNIZING THE NEED FOR CHANGE

A foundation of mutual trust is critical to ensure that breakdowns are productive stumbling blocks rather than complete collapse. Meyer underscores the role of secret or back-channel talks preceding official negotiations as an important means of creating trust. Talks about talks help prepare negotiators for talks about substance. "The process is equally important to content," he explains. "You can't expect to get a successful outcome if there hasn't been a successful process." For five years before the first official talks began in South Africa, high-level officials from both sides met regularly with Nelson Mandela in his prison cell to discuss the process and build trust and confidence in one another. Both sides would later draw upon this repository of trust when they encountered hurdles and breakdowns in negotiations.

During the negotiations, Meyer says this trust was a very important driving force—"the cement that kept the process on track, even in difficult times." The deposits of trust between Meyer and Cyril Ramaphosa, chief negotiator for the ANC, were critical to achieving breakthroughs at difficult times and ultimately helped them reach a settlement. In Meyer's view, this would have been impossible if the National Party and the ANC had not built mutual trust before the talks officially began.

"I viewed Roelf, not as a person, but as a member of the National Party, as an oppressor, as Deputy Minister of Police," recalls Mohammed Bhabha, who was one of the lead negotiators for the ANC. "He represented, in the abstract, everything we regarded as evil." But something happened when they encountered each other across the negotiating table. "It grew organically," Bhabha says, "we recognized the pragmatism, the genuineness. There's an inner morality in him that's extremely appealing."

Personal chemistry between leaders of opposing sides is also important. "It is important to recognize people who get along," Meyer advises. He believes that part

"Don't look for a Mandela.
Do what is
required yourselves."

of the reason he was appointed chief negotiator was because of his good relationship with Ramaphosa. Though there is no precise recipe for developing compatibility with another person, Meyer points to understanding as a key element. Understanding comes from getting to know the other person, evaluating and developing respect for that person. "Out of respect develops trust. You'd know by one or another stage in the process that he or she would not let you down. That is the real core of that chemistry."

THE PARADIGM SHIFT: EQUALITY MUST BE FOR ALL

But no amount of trust would have brought peaceful change to South Africa without a change in mindset, a paradigm shift. "The paradigm shift requires that you go full out, accept with an inner conviction," Meyer explains. "It's an emotional attachment that you have to learn, not only an intellectual realization. And unless you do that, you're not going to get to the other side of the paradigm." For the Afrikaner community, this meant turning upside

BOTTOM: President William Jefferson Clinton; Ambassador Nelson Santos, Permanent Representative of Timor-Leste to the United Nations; and Roelf Meyer at 2007 Project initiative, "Ready to Govern: Developing a Strategy for Kosovo's First 120 Days" held at the Pocantico Estate in 2007.

> "To change from the idea that 'I am better than the next person' to 'we are all equal' is a fundamental process involving emotion more than intellectual understanding. It involves deeply personal values and passions and has to come from the soul."

down centuries-old notions of racial superiority. "To change from the idea that 'I am better than the next person' to 'we are all equal' is a fundamental process involving emotion more than intellectual understanding. It involves deeply personal values and passions and has to come from the soul."

In Meyer's view, taking ownership is critical to this kind of paradigm shift and to successful conflict resolution. "We took ownership of the problem, of the design of the process, and eventually, of the outcome." The two sides collaborated to build a communications process that enabled them to talk to each other; according to Meyer, it worked because they built it together. The South African process was also very inclusive; not only were the two major parties engaged, but other, smaller parties of all affiliations were accommodated and welcome to join the process. "I think that helped us to reach, in the final instance, a settlement that was approved by everybody," Meyer says, "because people accepted the inclusive nature of the process." Involving everyone in the process also meant that everyone could take ownership of the outcome.

IT'S UP TO THE PEOPLE TO BRING ABOUT CHANGE THEMSELVES

Meyer recalls numerous conflicts in the last 15 years where outside intervention prevented people from taking ownership of their own situation and, as a result, the conflicts were not resolved. Without embracing a sense of ownership, it is impossible to experience the paradigm shift that Meyer believes is so critical to successful conflict resolution. The international community can exert all the pressure it has on a country, but if its people have not yet recognized the need for change, then no lasting progress will be made. "It's up to the people to do it themselves."

Perhaps surprisingly, Meyer does not consider leadership a top factor leading to change. Although leadership played an important role in South Africa, he has seen it have almost no effect in other countries. He often hears, "But we don't have a Mandela!" In response, he points to the power of transforming mindsets and building ownership and trust. "Don't look for a Mandela," he asserts, "do what is required yourselves."

GUATEMALA

1954 Carlos Castillo leads coup backed by the CIA after the nationalization of plantations of the United Fruit Company by President Jacobo Arbenz Guzman.

1960 Beginning of the civil war as left-wing guerrilla groups form and start battling government forces.

1966 After the election of President Montenegro, the Guatemalan army launches a successful counterinsurgency campaign that targets left-wing guerrilla groups in the mountains and rural areas. The 1970s see an escalation in violence.

1982 General Efrain Rios Montt seizes control of the government and voids the 1965 constitution, dissolves Congress and suspends all political parties. He forms local defense patrols in the countryside to reclaim the more indigenous areas.

1987-1994 José María Argueta co-founds and leads Centro ESTNA, bringing together key stakeholders from all sectors of Guatemalan society to recreate a shared national interest. In 1992, Argueta exports the ESTNA methodology to El-Salvador.

1994 President Jorge Serrano dissolves Congress and the Supreme Court and restricts civil liberties but is forced to resign. In his stead, the Human Rights Ombudsman, Ramiro de Leon Carpio, becomes President. Carpio charges Argueta with establishing the country's first civilian intelligence entity, appointing him as the National Security Adviser. Peace talks between the rebels and the government begin.

1996 Peace negotiations are finalized under a new President, Alvaro Arzu. Peace accords are signed in December.

1996-2000 Argueta serves as the ambassador to Peru, where he is taken hostage by MRTA guerrillas at the Japanese ambassador's residence. He helps lead the initial negotiations with the MRTA. Following the hostage crisis, Argueta serves as the ambassador to Japan for three years.

2011 Argueta is appointed as Secretary of Strategic Intelligence by President Otto Perez Molina.

JOSÉ MARÍA ARGUETA

Changing Mindsets

In a country ravaged by decades of brutal conflict and centuries of discrimination based on ethnicity, class and language, how can citizens find anything in common, let alone create a shared vision for their future? This was the fundamental challenge facing a deeply divided Guatemala during its long civil war, which broke out in the late 1960s and lasted more than 30 years. Though initially a conflict with a clear narrative about exclusion, property and ideology that pitted the ultra-rich landowning class against the country's destitute peasantry, Guatemala's civil war transformed into a hydra that dragged every sector of society into a vicious conflict operating on multiple fronts. The war fed off both local tensions and Cold War frictions, and fomented a national campaign of violent counterinsurgency carried out by the military primarily against the country's indigenous peoples. "It was a history that made no one proud," says José María Argueta, Guatemala's first civilian National Security Advisor and a founder of Centro ESTNA, the Center for Strategic Studies for National Stability.

DEVELOPING A SHARED NATIONAL IDENTITY

Civil war ripped Guatemala's social fabric to shreds. When the conflict finally ended, perhaps the only thing that all Guatemalans shared was exhaustion with war and a deep, generalized distrust built up over generations. No one trusted anyone, least of all long-time enemies and political rivals. In a population deeply scarred by a vicious war and poisoned by fear and distrust, what can help people to think beyond the needs of their own group and begin to consider the needs of the country as a whole? How do you build a society where different narratives and competing views about the future can coexist, where conflicts are mediated through democratic institutions and the rule of law, and people feel connected to each other by a common bond of citizenship in a shared state? Do leaders have a special responsibility to change the fear-hardened mindsets of their community? What does it take for leaders to begin to think differently, to think beyond the traditional, narrow mindset of class, caste and tribe, where another group's gain is your loss? And how can leaders be encouraged to consider the national interest instead of their own interests, so that they can help their nation move forward as one?

In 1985, Guatemala elected Vinicio Cerezo as its first civilian president in the country's first democratic election in over 20 years. Although the civil war still raged, there was widespread desire to end the violence and find a way toward peace, which was the country's only hope if it was ever to achieve stability and development.

Cerezo's government and some members of the military understood that the previous tactics of counterinsurgency were unsustainable and a strategic failure. It was time for a fresh examination of the causes and dynamics underlying Guatemala's decades of unresolved violence as a first step toward finding a way forward. It was in this context that Argueta was recruited to undertake a study for the Ministry of Defense that would provide a more nuanced understanding of the deep and persistent divisions within Guatemalan society. "When I mentioned that the first thing we needed to tackle was corruption," Argueta recalls, "and the Minister of Defense accepted that as something desirable, I knew that I could work with him."

Argueta already had firsthand experience with corruption. Trained as an economist, Argueta had previously worked at the Ministry of the Economy, where in the course of time he realized that several of the Ministry's highest officials were taking bribes. "I was brought up to understand what is right and what is wrong, and then to do what is right," Argueta says, so he was shocked by their greed and lack of integrity, which undermined the national interest. He went directly to the Minister of Economics with proof of his superiors' corruption. The Minister was skeptical, but promised to look into Argueta's claim. A few weeks later the Minister called Argueta in and told him that he had been awarded a scholarship to study for a Master's degree in Chile. Argueta's denunciation of his superiors went unmentioned. Faced with this brazen example of the power of corruption, Argueta resigned on the spot.

ALL CONFLICT IS DRIVEN BY EXCLUSION

In his new assignment for the Cerezo government, Argueta and a colleague travelled the country to identify the key sectors that constituted Guatemalan society and to meet with representatives of these communities to listen and learn about their perspectives on the conflict. Over the course of 18 months, they met with Mayan community leaders, local oligarchs, heads of large private-sector enterprises, labor leaders, members of the UNRG guerilla movement, women, religious leaders and members of the military and local and national government departments. At the end of this journey, Argueta returned with a simple message: all conflict is driven by exclusion.

"If you're excluded, you have no ability to pursue or promote your interests or that of the group you represent," Argueta explains. "That is the source of frustration, particularly because by being excluded you have no opportunity whatsoever to have a say on whatever decisions are being made that will affect your future." Over time, frustration over exclusion can build up and explode in violence. "On the psychological side, exclusion makes you feel vulnerable, and even threatened. That translates into fear," Agueta says. "Once fear kicks in, your reaction is going to be violent because then it becomes an issue of survival."

Argueta also noticed that while Guatemala had the trappings of a democratic system, all the groups that participated in or engaged with government distrusted

"If we are going to make an effort to bring people together, why don't we bring them together to try and define a dream they could all share?"

each other and perceived one another as competitors. Leaders of traditionally powerful groups, such as the economic elite and the military, used the systems of government to promote their own interests rather than the national interest. Argueta hypothesized that if a critical mass of leaders from all sectors of society started thinking about and working toward the interests of the country as a whole, then all Guatemalans could take ownership of the war and the country could achieve peace that would endure.

DEFINING A SHARED DREAM

In 1987, President Cerezo gave Argueta the chance to test his theories about creating shared interests and addressing exclusion to help consolidate Guatemala's democratic process. Argueta took a leading role in creating Centro ESTNA, which provided the first venue for Guatemalans of differing perspectives to get to know each other across the traditional divides, build relationships of trust and begin to think in terms of a shared national interest. ESTNA's core concept, Argueta explains, was that "if we are going to make an effort to bring people together, why don't we bring them together to try and define a dream they could all share?"

Trust had to be built into the ESTNA process from the outset, especially since it was established by the military, which gave many sectors of Guatemala's divided society severe misgivings. Argueta sought the blessings of two former presidents: Juan José Arévalo, leader of the 1944 democratic revolution, and Carlos Manuel Arana Osorio, the principal military strategist in the defeat of a rebel group in the early 1960s. Securing the joint endorsement of these two political

José María Argueta, first Civilian National Security Advisor of Guatemala, with Aleksander Kwaśniewski, Chairman of the Polish Social Democratic Party, in Warsaw in 1994.

José María Argueta, Guatemala's ambassador to Peru, just after his release from the Japanese Embassy after being held hostage for 10 days in 1996 by the Tupac Amaru Revolutionary Movement in Peru.

giants of the left and the right gave the ESTNA process the neutral authority to convene political dialogue on a range of divisive issues and helped to overcome mutual suspicions. ESTNA also strove to ensure that its participants were "true leaders" rather than close associates or relatives of those in power, and that they actually had the political will to participate in earnest.

Centro ESTNA brought together representatives of different sectors of Guatemalan society who had no tradition of dialogue, no mutual trust and no sense of shared responsibility for the fate of their country. Argueta says that a key challenge was: "How do we get these folks to speak their minds without insulting one another and without resorting to volence, which is what they are used to?" ESTNA sought to move beyond "the zero-sum mentality that emerges from fear produced by traditional ways of conducting business."

MOVING BEYOND A ZERO-SUM MENTALITY

ESTNA participants met regularly for nine months to develop a common vocabulary and a national perspective, and, eventually, to work together to find common solutions to national problems. According to Argueta, ESTNA "broke down the barriers of communication by ripping off titles and ranks"; participants addressed each other by their first names, human to human. Gradually other techniques fostered genuine dialogue. The participants went back to their constituents and shared what they were learning, and brought their constituents' feedback into their discussions. Little by little, Argueta says, all of their groups "were affected by the new mindset of the leadership." The important breakthrough comes, "when people begin to realize that somehow they have been part of the problem." This understanding "pushes them to be willing to be part of the solution."

Participants in ESTNA attest to its impact on their thinking. "Everyone agrees how valuable the experience was for opening their minds to new, diverse ideas," says Maurice Benard, Dean of the Faculty of Social and Political Sciences at Rafael Landivar University.

"One may not always reach agreement through dialogue," says another ESTNA participant, Adolfo Achilles Vela Galindo, "but it helps strengthen respect for and understanding of the ideas of others through communication." ESTNA helped Vela "reaffirm and strengthen my nationalism" and "understand that no state policy or law is inherently positive or valid unless it is based on the interests of the nation."

ESTNA's efforts helped spread change throughout Guatemala, with long-term effects. Guatemala emerged with a large cohort of top political leaders who not only were more familiar with the root causes and tensions inherent in their conflict, but, more important, they developed personal relationships across the political spectrum that they used to resolve national crises. The most dramatic example occurred in 1994, when ESTNA alums worked together to overturn a coup led by then President Jorge Serrano, who sought to consolidate power by abolishing the sitting congress and suspending the Constitution. One of the ESTNA graduates opposed to the coup, Otto Perez Molina, who was then Guatemala's Director of Intelligence, directly confronted the Minister of Defense, insisting that the role of the Army was not to overthrow the government but to protect the Constitution. A number of ESTNA alums who commanded military bases around the country backed Perez up. Their support for Perez quickly spread throughout the military, and other ESTNA graduates who were journalists, members of the clergy, businesspeople and labor leaders joined forces to thwart the coup. This was the first time in Guatemalan history that a coup was overturned.

SHARING ESTNA'S LESSONS

Because of its success in Guatemala, ESTNA soon became a model for neighboring El Salvador, where the US-backed military government and the Farabundo Marti National Liberation Front (FMLN), a coalition of left-wing guerilla groups, had been at war since the late 1970s. Argueta worked with Leonel Gómez, a Salvadoran human rights activist, to establish Centro Demos, an organization that promoted reconciliation by bringing together all sectors of society in a neutral

Tim Phillips, Chair of the Project; Angier Biddle Duke, Former ambassador to El Salvador; George Biddle, Vice President of the International Rescue Committee; President Jimmy Carter; and José María Argueta at 1994 Project initiative, "Reflections on Transition," in Managua.

> "We need to find ways
> in which people feel less excluded,
> ways in which they
> can actually be part of the
> decision making process."

space. Demos, which was launched in San Salvador in 1993 at a national event to foster reconciliation co-sponsored by the Project on Justice in Times of Transition, built on the concepts that had made ESTNA so successful: neutral dialogue and an inclusive approach. Its patron was Mauricio Gutiérrez, Chief Justice of the Salvadoran Supreme Court, whose involvement reassured El Salvador's right wing that Demos was balanced.

After helping to establish Centro Demos, Argueta returned to Guatemala to serve as the country's first civilian National Security Advisor. He was subsequently tapped to serve as Guatemala's ambassador to Peru, where in December 1996 he found himself one of over 30 diplomats taken hostage at the residence of the Japanese ambassador by guerillas from the Túpac Amaru Revolutionary Movement (MRTA). A member of the original negotiating team selected by the hostages to deal with their captors, Argueta used the skills he had honed leading ESTNA to secure their release.

Since the mid-1990s, Argueta has also helped leaders in Sri Lanka, Colombia and Iraq (mainly through the Project on Justice in Times of Transition) to better understand the obstacles to peace and the ways to create conditions conducive to changing entrenched mindsets and patterns of behavior, thereby allowing the development of a new, shared vision of a true national interest. In January 2012, Argueta was reappointed to his old job as Guatemala's National Security Advisor in the new administration of President Otto Perez Molina (who had led the opposition to the 1994 coup). He has once again taken to Guatemala's roads to assess the mood of the people and prospects for change during a period of escalating conflict. Today, the challenges and inequities of economic development, including corruption, are feeding into a persistent culture of violence. "The level of conflict has grown so much, exacerbated by folks who actually make a living on producing conflict. But it is all caused by the fact that communities are not informed," Argueta insists. "We need to find ways in which people feel less excluded and ways in which they can actually be part of the decision making process on things that will impact them directly." Especially when democracy is fragile and society has many fault lines, dialogue among all sides must be constant and must repeatedly ask, "What is it that brings us together as human beings? What do we have in common?" This will help to build the necessary trust and respect that can enable different factions to work together toward a national interest.

NORTHERN IRELAND

1920 Partition of Ireland, two parliaments are created (one in Dublin, one in Belfast).

1948 Creation of the Republic of Ireland, excluding the six northern counties which remain part of the United Kingdom.

1968 Bloody Sunday and the imposition of direct rule. British paratroopers fire on protestors demonstrating against internment and the ban on marches. The British government suspends the Northern Ireland government; Northern Ireland is to be ruled directly from London. In response, the Irish Republican Army (IRA) increases violence.

1985 Anglo-Irish Agreement: leaders of Britain and Ireland meet to discuss the situation, giving back some control of Northern Ireland to the Irish government. The agreement was never fully implemented.

1993 Downing Street Declaration: After talks between the British Prime Minister and the Irish leadership, it is declared that Northern Ireland can decide its own future and that Sinn Fein can have a seat if IRA violence is stopped. As a result, IRA declares a ceasefire in 1994.

1996 Monica McWilliams co-founds the Northern Ireland Women's Coalition.

1998 Belfast "Good Friday" Agreement: a settlement is reached, allowing for Northern Ireland to decide its own political status and whether its people consider themselves Irish or British. McWilliams is elected as a Member of Northern Ireland Assembly representing the Northern Ireland Women's Coalition.

2005-2011 McWilliams is appointed as the Chief Commissioner of the Northern Ireland Human Rights Commission.

MONICA MCWILLIAMS

Building Trust Among Enemies

When the peace process began in Northern Ireland in the early 1990s, Monica McWilliams was an academic, writing about the role of women in political conflict. Yet rather than keep her distance and observe the peace talks through the lens of the theoretical, McWilliams took a big risk and decided to make the leap from scholar to politician and bring a new perspective to the two hardened sides of the decades-long conflict. "Formal politics wasn't something that many of us wanted to spend our days on," McWilliams recalls. "It was very adversarial, tribal, there was very little productivity and little outcome." For a long time, she says, "I wanted nothing to do with it. I thought the pure stuff was all done outside. But then I realized listening to the South Africans at the 1995 Project on Justice in Times of Transition Belfast conference that you have to be inside politics to bring about real change." That was a decisive moment for McWilliams, one that prompted her to co-found the cross-community Northern Ireland Women's Coalition.

A NEW APPROACH TO POLITICS

The Women's Coalition was a departure from the traditional male-dominated politics of Northern Ireland, and it also declined to lend its support to any of the established political identies of Unionist, Nationalist or Republican. The Coalition brought a fresh perspective to the peace negotiations, which until then had been driven by competing Catholic and Protestant historical narratives, mutual suspicion and blame, and the constitutional issues surrounding British and Irish identity. McWilliams and her party saw an opportunity to discuss not just the words in the agreement, but what society would look like after the transition from conflict to peace: Would schools be desegregated? What would happen to all the weapons? "We felt there were added issues, and that if we weren't at the table, they wouldn't be on the agenda." The Coalition also knew that the limited role of women in public life had led to the conservative social policies that prevailed in Northern Ireland, and they wanted to make a change.

Monica McWilliams, founder of the Northern Ireland Women's Coalition, at 1999 Project initiative, "Strengthening the Role of Women in Bosnian Politics," held in Sarajevo.

The decision to enter the peace negotiations created turmoil both within and outside the Women's Coalition. Up to that point, the progress that Northern Ireland's women's movement had made in bringing the two sides together had been achieved outside politics by women—including McWilliams—who were peace and civil rights activists. Many of them had misgivings about McWilliams's decision to enter politics: "Everybody said, 'Are you mad? You're going to ruin your reputation!'" But the possibility that the peace negotiations could actually succeed was enough to overcome any doubts. "For the first time, you're going to have two governments at the table, the British and the Irish," McWilliams recalls. "You're going to have all the parties who were party to the problem at the table. So potentially, you had a very good mix to make a successful outcome."

The Northern Ireland Women's Coalition was not welcomed into the negotiations with open arms. "We were the new girls on the block," McWilliams says. "We were told practically every day that we shouldn't even be at the table." She describes her party as the "double other": Coalition members were seen as outsiders not only because they were women, but also because, by including Unionists, Nationalists, Catholics and

Protestants, they defied neat categorization. McWilliams and her colleagues had to work hard to get up to speed on what had already been discussed in the negotiations and the resulting outcomes. "Of course, they wanted to keep it all confidential, and nobody would tell us anything. That was part of the issue of trust."

AN ABSENCE OF TRUST

In her unique role as outsider on the inside, McWilliams was able to see problems more clearly than her more entrenched counterparts. Although no stranger to politics—she had been involved in community activism, human rights and women's rights—McWilliams quickly encountered the biggest obstacle plaguing the peace process: a lack of trust. She observed a complete absence of trust between the Unionists and Republicans. The Republicans wanted to be taken at their word that they were sincere about their ceasefire, but the Unionists heard only empty declarations. "You had a complete vacuum of understanding in the middle," says McWilliams. She compares it to her experience working with victims of domestic violence; abused women were told to trust their husbands because they had changed, "but they wouldn't trust him until they judged him by his actions, and whether he was going to take responsibility for his previous behavior." But unlike in a domestic relationship, in the peace process there was no foundation on which to build trust because there were no personal connections between the two sides. "People were strangers to each other."

Indeed, the opposing sides were barely civil to one another. "Many of them took pride in the fact that they hadn't ever said 'good morning' to each other and never would," McWilliams notes. People sitting across the table refused to look one another in the eye. When former US

Senator and chair of the negotiations George Mitchell encouraged the parties to work on building trust, "people used to yawn. They felt, and they actually said it, 'we are nowhere near getting to trust.'" The parties wanted to focus on agreeing on rules and procedure, and expected that trust would come later. "But we learned to our peril that actually we should have taken that head on and broken down what we meant by trust."

Word choice played a critical role in the negotiations. McWilliams explains that the parties were too cynical early on to even contemplate using the word "trust." "The language that people were using at the table wasn't the language of trust. It was very adversarial and bitter and untrustworthy." The word "trust" is still rarely used by politicians in Northern Ireland: "People talk about community relations, they talk about sharing, they talk about cohesion, they even talk about building human rights and social justice and equality, but they don't talk much about trust." McWilliams sees this as a sign of just how long it takes for people to grow comfortable not only with a word, but also with what they understand it to mean. Another word the parties struggled with during negotiations was "compromise," and whether it connoted strength or weakness. "We started using the word 'accommodation' instead of compromise, saying that we needed to reach an accommodation," McWilliams recalls. "And instead of trust we used the word 'confidence.' So we talked about 'confidence-building measures' instead of 'trust-building measures.'"

BREAKING DOWN BARRIERS AROUND THE DINNER TABLE

When political opponents can barely look at each other and "trust" becomes an unutterable word, it is

Monica McWilliams immediately following the signing of the Good Friday Agreement, April 10th 1998.

Shosh Arar, Israel City Women's Affairs Advisor to Benjamim Netanyahu; Monica McWilliams, founder of the Northern Ireland Women's Coalition; and Zahira Kamal, Ministry of Planning and International Cooperation of the Palestinian Authority, at 1999 Project initiative, "Strengthening the Role of Women in Bosnian Politics."

sometimes necessary to turn to outside support. In 1993, the Project on Justice in Times of Transition became involved with the Northern Ireland peace process, convening in 1995 a national gathering in Belfast on peace and reconciliation that featured leaders from South Africa, Eastern Europe and Latin America. Over the course of a decade, the Project conducted 18 initiatives for Northern Ireland's parties at key moments in the peace process. These included several workshops at Harvard's Kennedy School of Government in which participants studied other conflicts, which gradually enabled them to extend their discussions to their own conflict. For the first time, in the safe, neutral space of an American university, McWilliams unexpectedly heard her counterparts "saying things that were actually quite thoughtful. Despite the stubbornness they showed

at home, in this setting they conveyed openness and a willingness to start working together."

"I have learned that if you want people to sit down, you look them in the face, you look them in the eye, you try and eat a little bit of dinner together," she says. "It was impossible for us to do that in Northern Ireland, not just because our communities were segregated and our talks were segregated, but there was no way that we could actually debrief in this way over dinner." Gradually, the participants began to feel the effect of being away from Northern Ireland, out of the eye of the local media, away from the pressures of their constituencies, and they began to communicate with each other. Up to that point they had been total strangers: "People preferred to remain like that, they thought that was a great strength." For the first time they were able to find out about each other's lives.

> "When political opponents can barely look at each other and "trust" becomes an unutterable word, it is sometimes necessary to turn to outside support."

McWilliams also took part in an important meeting hosted by South Africa in 1997 in which representatives of all the Northern Ireland parties met with the South African leaders who had managed to broker peace despite the odds. At that point, the Unionists and Republicans refused to be in the same room with each other. "Mandela had to do his talk twice as a result," McWilliams says. "He told us that we had brought Apartheid to South Africa after Apartheid had ended! We were quite ashamed when he said that, and so we should have been, because we had to have two of everything. Two men's toilets, two dining rooms, two sets of planes, two buses to take us everywhere: two of everything." This trip to South Africa and subsequent Project meetings in other countries that had experienced conflict and worked through it, not only provided insight, but also provided safe space and distance. "We couldn't have done it without being brought outside to places that were safe and private, where there was unbelievable hospitality," says McWilliams. "Eventually, given the frozen state that we were in, we could only start to melt."

THE VIEW FROM THE BALCONY

Despite considerable cracks in the icy demeanor of the two sides, keeping their own communities happy while also bringing them along on the path to peace constantly challenged all the parties. "When you speak, you represent a constituency, but you're also trying to make peace, so you're having to speak to the other constituency. But if you're going to get elected again, you better make bloody sure that the people who are voting for you . . . do they want to hear this? It is a really, really difficult thing."

McWilliams recalls an experience that nearly destroyed her party. The Women's Coalition took pride in not identifying as Unionist, Nationalist or Republican, but rather as "inclusive other." In 1998, there was a vote to make David Trimble of the Ulster Unionist Party First Minister of Northern Ireland, but he needed the pledge of three more Unionists to gain the post. Trimble's election was critical to the continuation of the peace process because of the central role he played on the Unionist side. "We re-designated in order to lend our vote to him and one of us became a Unionist and the other became a Nationalist for a day. We did this to show that it was possible for another party to lend him two of their votes so that the governance arrangements could be established, and that is exactly what happened at that time," McWilliams affirms. Women's Coalition members were furious that the leadership of their cross-community party would align itself with the Unionist side. "But we said, 'Look, this is bigger than our party, this is actually something

"Very late in the day, we were able
to understand what Cyril Ramaphosa and
Roelf Meyer had been telling us since
the first Project initiative in 1995, which was
to pick up the phone to each other."

we need to do for the sustainability of this Assembly and for the peace agreement and for the country. If the party suffers, so be it.'"

As leader of the Women's Coalition, McWilliams was constantly being questioned by members of her own party about why she did certain things that were not what they had expected. "Sometimes during those negotiations, trust had to be built internally as well as externally," she explains, noting that she made a point of communicating with her constituents to keep them informed and on the same page. She also emphasizes that "if there were more interaction between our politicians and civil society, they would help each other—it would bring a greater level of understanding which would create a greater strength in the peace process."

Keeping the greater goal in mind is critical to resolving conflicts, but this ability to "get on the balcony" and look out over the whole scene is all too rare. "When you're in conflict you tend to end up contemplating your own belly button, rather than

looking upwards and outwards to where you want to be going," McWilliams states. "That's why peace negotiators end up focusing on the tiniest of details rather than on the big transitional issues." They need to be reminded that they are working toward a shared goal that will benefit all their communities. This is why open lines of communication—and trust—matter so much.

"Very late in the day, we were able to understand what Cyril Ramaphosa and Roelf Meyer had been telling us since the first Project initiative in 1995, which was to pick up the phone to each other," McWilliams relates. These two South African negotiators from opposing sides emphasized the importance of building personal relationships, "seeing the humanity in the other person," and communicating and reaching out through difficult times. "It took us a few years to get there," McWilliams notes, "because people were much more fixated on getting the paperwork right and the words right on paper than they were on getting the words right in their own personal language toward one another. But things have changed phenomenally."

ISRAEL/PALESTINE

1948 British Mandate in Palestine ends. War breaks out between Jewish and Arab communities in Palestine while Arab armies invade. The State of Israel is created.

1967 The Six-Day War. In a preemptive strike, Israel conquers the West Bank, the Sinai and the Golan Heights in six days.

1973 The Yom-Kippur or October War. In a surprise attack on the Jewish holiday of Yom Kippur, Arab countries led by Syria and Egypt attempt to retake the Sinai and Golan. The status quo ante bellum is ultimately maintained.

1977 Egyptian President Anwar Sadat visits the Israeli Knesset. Egyptian-Israeli peace treaty is subsequently signed.

1987-1993 First Palestinian Intifada: a popular uprising against the Israeli occupation of the West Bank and Gaza.

1992-2003 Naomi Chazan serves as Member of the Knesset on behalf of the Meretz Party, including as Deputy Speaker of the Knesset from 1996 onward.

1993 Oslo Accords signed, establishing mutual recognition between the State of Israel and the Palestine Liberation Organization. Peace process starts. Chazan is heavily involved in people-to-people initiatives, such as Jerusalem Link, Bat Shalom and the International Women's Commission for Israeli-Palestinian Peace.

1995 Israeli Prime Minister Yitzhak Rabin is assassinated by right-wing Jewish extremist.

2000-2004 Following failure of the peace process, the second Palestinian Intifada breaks out.

2008-2009 Gaza War refocuses international attention on the conflict.

2008-2012 Chazan serves as the head of the New Israel Fund, an organization that supports civil society and human rights organizations within Israel.

NAOMI CHAZAN

Compromising with the Other

By the late 1990s, the Israeli parlimentarian and peace advocate Naomi Chazan was "totally convinced" that many political conflicts around the globe were "more intractable than the Israel-Palestine issue." At the time, an Israeli-Palestinian peace agreement seemed inevitable, within reach. Israelis and Palestinians at all levels of public and private life were regularly meeting with one another, together trying to "find ways of sharing the land, of achieving dignity without eradicating the other." Chazan has always believed that respecting the values and identity of the other side is a prerequisite for negotiations and eventually a compromise. "If you ignore or belittle the other's identity and values, it won't work. You have to accept that as a starting point, as something that has to be respected." Accepting the identity of the other side as a given opens the way for dialogue because it grounds you in the present: "If you accept the legitimacy of the other side and the way the other side defines its identity, then you should be accepting the fact that people are responsible for what's happening and not history, and not religion."

TALKING IS ALWAYS BETTER

The era of the Oslo peace process was a time of hope and change. But spoilers and mismanagement on both sides led to collapse, violence and separation. "Compromise" became a dirty word, evoking surrender, betrayal and weakness. In the past decade, as Chazan bluntly puts it, "nobody is happy. Never in my life have I seen two more depressed societies." In this radicalizing, dark environment, Chazan's persistence is important. Drawing on the lessons of this harsh reality, Chazan has a deep and nuanced understanding of how to achieve compromise without calling for the other to change identity.

"Part of the problem of this fear of compromise is that people are afraid of losing themselves when they are dealing with the other," Chazan maintains. Having spent her entire adult life promoting reconciliation between Israelis and Palestinians, she is intimately

Mr. Salvador Sanabria, representative of the Farabundo Marti National Liberation Front (FMLN) of El Salvador; Naomi Chazan, former Deputy Speaker of the Knesset, Israel; Zahira Kamal, Ministry of Planning and International Cooperation, Palestinian Authority; and Sir John Birch, Director of the British Association for Central and Eastern Europe, at 1997 Project initiative, "The Dynamics of Building Trust: Workshops to Strengthen Dialogue in Bosnia" in Mostar.

"*Enemy* is an abstract concept, sitting across from a *person* is different."

familiar with the essential ingredients—and dangerous misperceptions—of compromise. Schooled by successes and failures, by domestic and international experience, Chazan has developed a pragmatic view of compromise, one that informs her conduct and her work. Her approach demands courage, an unfaltering commitment to dialogue and discourse, and the belief that living in a democracy means "you should talk to everybody, and talking is always better."

This approach, in many ways, is part of Chazan's upbringing, a heritage and a birthright. Her parents, who immigrated to then Mandatory Palestine from London in the 1930s, were founding members of the civil service of the fledgling Israeli democracy, particularly its Ministry of Foreign Affairs. "My parents came to the land of Israel to live in a free nation. They came from a place of civil rights and human dignity, of respecting the other," she recalls. "They understood that a plurality of opinions only strengthens and steels." Chazan's commitment to democratic dialogue is innate: "democracy does not exist without opposition."

FEAR AS AN OBSTACLE TO PEACE

Chazan's support for dialogue with the Palestinians has provoked harsh public criticism, and without a clear political horizon, it is "now being brought into question by reality." For many, since the government erected a barrier between Israel and the occupied territories, the two-state solution has come to seem impossible. Chazan identifies fear as a debilitating obstacle to peace: "Both communities feel victimized by the other because of fear. I mean real, intense, profound fear, which is difficult sometimes even to convey." This fear has rendered many on both

sides incapable of empathizing, let alone interacting or compromising, with the other side. "We are back where we were 50 years ago," Chazan insists, "because we have lost the capacity to treat the other as a human being with similar needs and desires and aspirations as we have."

Chazan is under no illusion that a secret formula for peace exists. By definition, she says, "compromise means giving up something that is valuable," and it is neither easy nor pleasant. In the context of an intractable conflict like the Israeli-Palestinian one, everything becomes valuable. The problem worsens when "certain stances become elevated to the level of value or they become messianic." Many spoilers on both sides have done precisely that. Motivated by religiously inspired visions of the future, they have elevated sovereignty over a piece of land to the level of the sacred. For them, any territorial compromise constitutes sacrilege—a relinquishing of collective identity. Simply meeting with the other means compromising who you are. This completely precludes negotiations. "Once you are in a messianic situation you really can't negotiate because we haven't figured out a way to negotiate with the divine yet."

Naomi Chazan with Ambassador Nicholas Burns, former Under Secretary of State for Political Affairs at the US State Department, during 2009 Project class, "The Role of Leadership in Conflict Transformation."

Zahira Kamal, Ministry of Planning and International Cooperation, Palestinian Authority; Nik Gowing, broadcaster, BBC; and Naomi Chazan, former Deputy Speaker of the Knesset, in London at 1996 Project "Workshop on Reconciliation for Bosnia."

COMPROMISE AS A PRACTICAL NECESSITY

In Chazan's mind, the idea that negotiations will alter one's sense of identity is illogical. "You are not negotiating history, values or identities: you are instead negotiating interests and needs. You are negotiating your ability to fulfill your dreams." Once people understand that, she says, once they recognize that "they are not losing themselves at all," then they will find it "much easier to compromise on very specific substantive issues." Compromise is a "practical necessity," a way of affirming, rather than forfeiting, collective identities: "Compromise for me is a fairly utilitarian mechanism for advancing objectives and creating spaces so that everybody can essentially be themselves."

The main question now is how to convince Palestinian and Israeli publics and leaders to move forward. How does one reintroduce empathy in a time of near-complete separation? Chazan says persistence and innovation are paramount. In the face of a conflict that constantly evolves, "new levels and new layers are added, and

you have to deal with many more factors." Persistence is critical. But it "has to come together with constant innovation," says Chazan, because "the conflict itself has new dimensions being added."

VALUING HUMAN BEINGS, LIFE AND DIGNITY

Bolstered by decades of experience and great familiarity with failure, Chazan has some clear ideas on how to move forward. Certain activities must take place, for example, formulating a clear vision and taking small but practical steps. "You can't move forward unless you know where you're going, and therefore you have to have some sort of political vision of the nature of the resolution of the conflict." Once the vision is set, facilitating interaction between the two sides must be the next step. "You can't begin to move forward unless people are meeting and talking to each other." Simply sitting across the table from the other can make a huge difference in creating empathy and opening the door to compromise: "*Enemy* is an abstract concept, sitting across from a *person* is different."

Chazan also highlights the importance of inclusivity. Managing a peace process "cannot be just top-down, it's not going to work. It's got to come from the side and from the bottom as well." While she recognizes the need for discretion and high-level meetings, especially in the spoiler-rife landscape of Israeli-Palestinian negotiations, she insists that including the publics is a crucial ingredient to success. "Not every agreement has to be done in a closed room, because, you know, there's a real world out there. That's why Northern Ireland and South Africa are such good examples, because there was an attempt to consult constantly, to make people a part of the process."

"I never saw compromise in the negative," says Naomi Chazan. Perhaps she is in the minority now, but she hopes that others can begin to see the advantages of her brand of compromise, one based on valuing "human beings, life and dignity." Chazan has seen people in Northern Ireland and the Balkans find that what they thought was valuable is "actually something that is really not all that valuable and can even be an obstacle to the promotion of objectives and the realization of identities." Now she wants to revive this mindset in her own country. "For my entire adult life I have been a key advocate of a two-state solution, because I think that Israeli self-determination cannot be fully achieved without the self-determination of Palestinians," she says. "The most democratic, just and humane thing to do is have there be two states side by side." Neither side would lose its identity or values by agreeing to a compromise.

General Jovan Divjak and Naomi Chazan in Sarajevo during 1997 Project initiative, "The Dynamics of Building Trust: Workshops to Strengthen Dialogue in Bosnia."

CHILE

1970 Salvador Allende, a Marxist, is elected to the presidency and begins a series of radical social reform.

1973 Gen. Augusto Pinochet mounts a CIA backed coup, overthrows Allende and begins a brutal dictatorship. At the same time, José Zalaquett heads the Human Rights Department of the Committee for Peace in Chile that provided legal assistance to thousands of political prisoners and their families.

1975-1986 Zalaquett is imprisoned for his human rights work and subsequently sent into exile in 1976. During this time he serves on the Executive Committee of Amnesty International. In 1986, he is allowed to return.

1988 Gen. Pinochet loses a referendum on whether he should remain in power.

1989 Christian Democrat Patricio Aylwin is elected president and the transition to democracy begins with the implementation of 54 constitutional reforms.

1990 Gen. Pinochet steps down as head of state but remains commander-in-chief of the army. Zalaquett is appointed to serve on the National Commission for Truth and Reconciliation which investigated human rights violations by the military-backed regime.

2000 Pinochet returns to Chile after being arrested in Britain for human rights abuses on a universal jurisdiction principle.

Confronting the Past and Forging a Shared Vision for the Future

"If you close a wound without cleaning it, it will fester and reappear," asserts the human rights lawyer José Zalaquett Daher, who has long been a staunch advocate of seeking the truth about crimes and abuses committed in both his native Chile and other countries emerging from violence and repression. As a member of Chile's National Commission for Truth and Reconciliation, Zalaquett grappled with the challenge of finding a balance between truth and justice in order to sustain peace and bolster democracy as Chile emerged from the grim years of the Pinochet military dictatorship.

A NATIONAL SECURITY RISK

Zalaquett's personal history is intimately linked with that of his homeland. In September 1973, the Chilean military violently overthrew one of Latin America's few longstanding democracies by seizing power from the government of President Salvador Allende. The state-sponsored violence carried out under the military junta headed by General Augusto Pinochet resulted in massive, systematic human rights abuses. Thousands of Chileans, including politicians, civil society activists, students and professionals, were imprisoned, tortured, killed or "disappeared" in the name of national security. A further 200,000 went into political exile abroad. In a small country like Chile, almost everyone knew someone who had been personally affected by political violence.

At the time of the coup, Zalaquett, a lawyer who had served as a minister in President Allende's cabinet, went to work for the interfaith Committee for Peace, which provided assistance to thousands of political prisoners and their families. Zalaquett himself was imprisoned twice, in 1975 and 1976. "No charges were brought against me. I was just considered a national security risk," he says.

"Being in prison is a source of anguish, particularly if you don't know how long you will be held in custody," Zalaquett relates. "Yet I was not tortured, so compared with the suffering of many others, I did not go through a lot." Following his second imprisonment, Zalaquett was expelled from his homeland. "Police officers escorted me

Participants at 1994 Project initiative, "Dealing with the Past," held in Cape Town, South Africa.

from prison to the airport and I was sent abroad. I landed in Paris." Less than a year later, he moved to the United States and headed the London-based international executive committee of Amnesty International. "During my exile, harsh as it was to be banned from my country, I feel I was lucky, because I learned a lot by becoming associated with the international human rights movement," says Zalaquett. "In retrospect, I may say that the pain is gone and the gains are still with me."

In 1986, Zalaquett was permitted to return to Chile. In 1988, in the face of a severe economic crisis and widespread civil resistance, the military junta authorized a plebiscite to allow the Chilean people to determine whether Pinochet's presidency should end. He was voted out of office and, in 1989, Patricio Aylwin was democratically elected president (though Pinochet retained the post of commander-in-chief). President Aylwin played an instrumental role in the restoration of democracy and the promotion of national reconciliation in Chile. As part of this process, in 1990, he established a National Commission for Truth and Reconciliation which was charged with investigating

and reporting to the nation on the worst human rights abuses committed under Pinochet. "The purpose of the Commission," according to Zalaquett, "was to produce an unimpeachable report about crimes that a good deal of society didn't believe existed, or needed to not believe existed in order to live at peace with their own conscience."

Zalaquett was appointed one of the Commission's eight members. "I was gratified to have the chance to provide some redress and to show respect for the relatives of so many people disappeared and killed," he says of his service on the Commission. "For many years prior to the establishment of the commission, they had been systematically shunned and ridiculed by the military authorities when they demanded to know the fate or whereabouts of their loved ones."

ALL THE TRUTH, AND AS MUCH JUSTICE AS POSSIBLE

Seeking the truth about past abuses is essential to national reconciliation, Zalaquett insists. "Since truth is part of memory, and memory is part of identity, a divided version of very key facts—morally relevant facts—would be like having a schizophrenic society with a divided identity," he says. "Truth is the initial step that opens the gate for further methods of reparation, of acknowledgment and justice." But Zalaquett is pragmatic, and he emphasizes that both a moral and a practical approach are necessary in dealing with past crimes. In his view, societies in transition from repression to democracy or from civil conflict to peace should seek "all the truth, and as much justice as possible."

"Justice can never be fully achieved for every single act," Zalaquett says. "Justice depends on factors that are not so easy to handle. Namely, the resistance of the perpetrators and the sheer difficulty of conducting many thousands of individual fair trials." The challenge is to balance the need to prosecute atrocities with the need to keep the peace. "Truth may be achieved," Zalaquett notes, "but not the whole truth, in the sense of the interpretive truth. That cannot be imposed." But it *is* possible to determine the truth about specific facts without establishing the guilt or innocence of alleged perpetrators. This is where a truth commission, which is an ethical panel rather than a court of law, can play a critical role.

Sometimes the facts of past crimes are known to everyone but not acknowledged. In polarized societies where many people still feel a sense of allegiance to the former regime, "a good section of the population denies basic facts, and you have to put the light on the table," Zalaquett explains. In his view, that is the main purpose of a truth commission. "When the truth is known, but not put on the table, not put in the annals of the nation, it may produce tensions because people may not feel recognized in their dignity and their identity." Zalaquett insists that it is essential "to acknowledge, rather than just to know, that these facts have a moral relevance, that these atrocities should never have happened, and express a resolution that they won't happen again." Thus the truth must be established by official means, and the government must acknowledge the truth.

José Zalaquett at 1993 Project initiative, "Democratization and Decommunization: Disqualification Measures in Eastern and Central Europe and the former Soviet Union," held in Venice, Italy.

INSPIRATION FOR SOUTH AFRICA

In 1994, on the eve of South Africa's first free elections, which would sweep away white-minority rule, the Project on Justice in Times of Transition brought Zalaquett and other Latin American and East European leaders to South Africa to share their experiences and approaches to dealing with the abuses of prior regimes. Zalaquett's contribution and the model of the Latin American truth commissions had the greatest resonance for the South Africans, who were struggling to find a way to deal with the horrible legacies of Apartheid while promoting reconciliation in the spirit of the peace accords and advancing the vision of a just and equal society for whites and blacks in the new South Africa as envisioned by Nelson Mandela. The Project and its local partners convened a follow-up conference that brought Zalaquett, President Alywin and other eminent Chileans to meet with their South African counterparts, and Zalaquett hosted a delegation of South Africans to meet with Chileans across the political spectrum to help them to further refine their thinking on how best to deal with the past.

Chile was the first to use the name "truth and reconciliation" for its commission, suggesting that the whole exercise had the ultimate purpose of achieving national reconciliation, which did not mean society would be free of conflict, but that its people could agree on some basic tenets of living together. "The South Africans liked that and they adopted the name," Zalaquett says. "This suggested to the public that the whole exercise is aimed at creating a society where there is some basic social contract, some basic agreement, particularly on the issue of respect for fundamental rights for everyone."

"In South Africa, everybody knew the facts of Apartheid," Zalaquett notes. "What the Truth and Reconciliation Commission concentrated on were the major crimes committed under the laws of Apartheid. The purpose was not to produce a package of

"You have to pursue an ideal of justice, and at the same time you have to navigate real-life difficulties to maximize the possibility of achieving the best possible outcome without risking the whole endeavor."

information that could be presented with great fanfare for the knowledge of everyone, like we did in Chile and Argentina," because everybody already knew what had gone on under Apartheid. Instead, "the purpose was to concentrate on the process and to give a voice to the people who had been denied a voice up until that point."

The South African Truth and Reconciliation Commission televised its proceedings, which, according to Zalaquett, "would have been impossible in Chile or Argentina." Open hearings are not always appropriate for truth commissions, he asserts; it depends on the purpose of the commission. "In Argentina and Chile, the purpose was to convince even the reluctant members of society, who had supported the military coups, that torture had happened." But because the aim of South Africa's Truth and Reconciliation Commission was "to give a voice to the people who had suffered so much," broadcasting its hearings was very important.

BALANCING JUSTICE AND RECONCILIATION

"I believe that a balance may be found between the need for justice and the desirability of reconciliation," Zalaquett says, but he is adamant that each country must find its own way to confront past crimes on the basis of its own realities. There is no universal approach. The South Africans, for example, "fashioned the whole exercise of the truth commission in their own manner, rather than attempting to copy the examples that they had studied." While it is important to learn from the experience of others, "every country needs to examine its own reality to see what kind of general lessons can apply, because there are no easy formulas." The main lesson is that "you have to keep a fresh mind, asking the questions anew in every situation. It's difficult to do that when there is a whole world of examples to draw from, but that's the challenge."

Zalaquett is concerned about the expansion of truth commissions to cover all kinds of things. "I'm not saying that you should have truth commissions only in the case of massive disappearances, but that

OPPOSITE: Project initiative, "Reconciliation in Times of Transition," held in 1993 in San Salvador. ABOVE: José Zalaquett at 1993 Project initiative held in Venice, Italy, "Democratization and Decommunization: Disqualification Measures in Eastern and Central Europe and the former Soviet Union."

> "You can find ways—
> to use the words of a poet—to unchop a tree,
> to bring a broken society back
> to its feet and to create or recreate a
> different, viable, just society."

certainly is one key undisputed situation where a truth commission may be needed." In his view, "the whole field of 'transitional justice' has become to some extent a kind of franchise or industry. If there's a problem, people think of establishing a truth commission without much ado, without much reflection about what needs to be addressed." He also objects to the term "transitional justice" because "it suggests that justice itself may be transient. And further, it suggests that the whole purpose is about justice, rather than a panoply of measures, including acknowledgment, memory preservation, truth telling, justice and, ultimately, reconciliation."

UNCHOPPING A TREE

Zalaquett points out an intrinsic challenge in the seeming impossibility of reconciling two valid moral propositions when dealing with past human rights abuses. On the one hand, "individual responsibility is paramount, so people should be accountable. On the other is the situation of polarization and division from over-zealous blame seeking, where there is a tendency for the worst in all of us to emerge. If you have too much of the latter, you fall into what the French call, 'to explain everything is to pardon everything.' But if you fall too much in the former, you fail to recognize

the reality of the fact that at one point, the whole nation may go crazy. So how to reconcile these two? I don't have a clue, I can only identify the problem." In his own case, Zalaquett has found his way to balance these contradictory tensions: "Without in any way relinquishing the principle of individual responsibility, I do not hold a grudge against most perpetrators."

Zalaquett is convinced that reconciliation is possible, and, in his role as a professor of human rights at the law schools of such leading universities as Harvard, the University of Toronto, the University of Maryland and, currently, the University of Chile, Zalaquett is training a new generation of law students to think critically about how human rights principles can best be upheld. The ultimate goal must always be achieving sustainable peace; justice should not be pursued at the expense of peace. "You have to pursue an ideal of justice, and at the same time you have to navigate real-life difficulties to maximize the possibility of achieving the best possible outcome without risking the whole endeavor." It is both a moral and political challenge. But Zalaquett remains adamant that in the wake of massive human rights abuses, war crimes or crimes against humanity, "you can find ways—to use the words of a poet—to unchop a tree, to bring a broken society back to its feet and to create or recreate a different, viable, just society."

The Project on Justice in Times of Transition: 20 Years of Putting Experience to Work for Peace

CENTRAL AND EASTERN EUROPE 1992–1995

The Project on Justice in Times of Transition was created in response to the collapse of communism in Eastern and Central Europe and the Soviet Union. Its initial programming focused on helping the newly established democracies address the difficult legacies of dictatorship and human rights violations as well as the toxic heritage of state security intimidation and abuses. The Project brought leaders from throughout the region and the United States together with individuals from other countries that had faced similar challenges. These included, among others, Aleksander Kwaśniewski, Joachim Gauck, Árpád Göncz, Jan Urban, Martin Bútora, Adam Michnik, Michael Žantovský, Jan Bielecki, Sergei Kovalev, Aleksander Smolar, József Szájer, Kurt Biedenkopf, Raúl Alfonsín, José Zalaquett, Rafael Michelini, Jorge Correa, Carlos Nino, Karel Schwarzenberg, Jacques Rupnik, Aryeh Neier, Jeri Laber, Lawrence Weschler, Neil Kritz, Stephen Holmes, Samuel Huntington, Ruti Teitel, Deborah Harding and Tina Rosenberg.

ACCOMPLISHMENTS

■ Organized the first conferences in Central and Eastern Europe and the former Soviet Union to address the legacy of communism and introduced a series of recommendations or "principles" that were adopted throughout the region dealing with human rights violations, the use of state security files, the challenge of dealing with collaborators of the former regimes, intelligence reform and larger issues of transitional justice and accountability.

■ Credited with launching the field of transitional justice at our inaugural conference in Salzburg in February of 1992 and through our subsequent meetings in East and Central Europe in the early 1990s.

EASTERN EUROPE

"The Project creates a kind of snowball effect, because it links people together and creates partnerships which continue long after the program has ended. The Project organizes conferences that focus on a wide range of issues and are responsive to the needs of each country, and the follow-up programs that are developed afterwards keep the momentum going…"

—JAN BIELECKI, FORMER PRIME MINISTER OF POLAND

INITIATIVES

■ **Justice in Times of Transition** *(Salzburg, Austria, 1992)* Launched the ongoing Project on Justice in Times of Transition; senior policy-makers from Europe, the former Soviet Union, Latin America and the United States examined experiences with "lustration" laws, the opening of police files to public scrutiny and committees of inquiry into the abuses of past regimes.

■ **Truth and Justice: The Delicate Balance** *(Budapest, Hungary, 1992)* Policy-makers, archivists and other experts from former communist countries discussed the status of security files in their countries and identified means of preventing the past from continuing to divide and control society.

■ **Democracy and Decommunization: Disqualification Measures in Eastern and Central Europe and the former Soviet Union** *(Venice, Italy, 1993)* Representatives from four continents (22 countries) evaluated a spectrum of legislation enacted as part of decommunization and considered "model principles" designed to inform future disqualification measures.

■ **Freedom and Expression in the Post-Communist System** *(Tirana, Albania, 1994)* Addressed the role of the free press in fragile democracies of East and Central Europe.

■ **Security Services in a Civil Society: Oversight and Accountability** *(Warsaw, Poland, 1995)* Explored means of ensuring that police and security agencies' mandates meet states' legitimate security needs in a way consistent with democratic principles.

ABOVE: "Democracy and Decommunization," Venice, Italy, 1993. BELOW: Marek Nowicki, Helsinki Foundation for Human Rights, and Tim Phillips, Project Chair, at "Security Services in Civil Society," Warsaw, Poland, 1995. OPPOSITE, TOP: Wendy Luers, Václav Havel, Peter Petri, William Luers and Prince Karel Schwarzenberg the day after Havel's inauguration. OPPOSITE, BOTTOM: Prince Karel Schwarzenberg, President Havel after Project meeting, "Justice in Times of Transition," Salzburg, 1992.

KOSOVO
2003–2012

In 2003, Prime Minister Bajram Rexhepi invited the Project on Justice in Times of Transition to Kosovo to help Kosovar Albanian leaders prepare for negotiations with Serbia and the United Nations over Kosovo's future status. The Project worked with both Kosovar Albanian and Serb leaders to help them build leadership skills and develop the capacity they would need to achieve stability in Kosovo and across the wider region. Eventually the Project also helped them to tackle key challenges that Kosovo faced as an emerging nation, from the status of minorities to the structure of local government and the status of northern Kosovo. Among the outside leaders the Project brought to Kosovo were: David Ervine, a former paramilitary and leader of the Progressive Unionist Party in the Northern Ireland Assembly; Roelf Meyer, former Chief Negotiator for F.W. de Klerk; Milorad Pupovac, Serb minority leader in the Croatian parliament; and Ashraf Ghani, former minister of finance and senior advisor to Afghan President Hamid Karzai. President William Jefferson Clinton, former Secretary of State Madeleine Albright, senior US diplomat Richard Holbrooke and senior US diplomat Frank Wisner were also active participants in Project initiatives related to Kosovo.

ABOVE: Prime Minister Çeku, President Clinton and President Sejdiu at "Ready to Govern: Developing a Strategy for Kosovo's First 120 Days," Pocantico, New York, 2007. OPPOSITE: Ramush Haradinaj, head of the AAK; Nexhat Daci, Speaker of the Assembly; President Rugova; Hashim Thaci, leader of the PDK; and Prime Minister Rexhepi at "Crafting Strategies for Negotiation," Burg Schlaining, Austria, 2003.

ACCOMPLISHMENTS

■ Convened several high-level meetings with senior Albanian and Serb leaders of Kosovo to consider the future of independence, democratic governance and reform. The Project's 2003 meeting in Austria was the first to bring together all five Kosvar Albanian leaders to consider a roadmap for Kosovo's future. The historic 2007 meeting at the Pocantico Estate in New York led to the signing of the "Pocantico Declaration" that laid out a unified vision for the future of an independent and democratic Kosovo and included top US and European leaders including President Clinton, Madeleine Albright, Richard Holbrooke, Nicholas Burns and Wolfgang Petritsch, among others.

■ Played a key role in promoting negotiations towards peace, reconciliation and transitional justice in Kosovo.

"In Kosovo, it was important to convey to the Kosovar Serb and Albanian leaders that there is a way forward, that you are not unique in your problems, and that other countries have gone through equally difficult challenges. The Project brought leaders from elsewhere with extraordinary personal experience who conveyed the message that change is possible and can be achieved together."

—Wolfgang Petrisch, former High Representative to Bosnia and Herzegovina and EU Representative to the Rambouillet talks

INITIATIVES

■ **Crafting Strategies for Negotiation** *(Burg Schlaining, Austria, 2003)* Brought together 15 senior leaders of the Kosovar Provisional Self Government to provide comparative perspectives from other transitional contexts on preparing for negotiations.

■ **Crafting Strategies for Negotiation and Effective Engagement** *(Vienna, Austria, 2004)* Brought together 14 senior Serb leaders in Kosovo to provide comparative perspectives from other transitional contexts on preparing for negotiations and power-sharing arrangements.

■ **Developing a Vision for the Future** *(Rahovec, Kaminice and Prizren, 2005)* Held three municipal meetings with political and community leaders in Kosovo to jump start discussion among them about how to go about strengthening local government institutions in the region. Discussions in these municipalities were facilitated with the help of mayors and NGO leaders from other Balkan countries.

■ **Ready to Govern: Developing a Strategy for Kosovo's First 120 Days** *(Pocantico Estate, New York, 2007)* Facilitated a several day retreat for senior members of the Kosovar government to consider the logistics involved in implementing the Ahtisaari Plan during the first 120 days after a UN resolution on the region's status. The Pocantico meeting ended with the Pocantico Declaration, which facilitated on-going collaboration between Unity Team members in the months prior to Independence.

■ **Ready to Govern: Preparing for Independence** *(Kosovo, 2007)* A strategic engagement which brought Ashraf Ghani (former Afghan Minister of Finance), Roelf Meyer (former Minister of Constitutional Affairs) and John Podesta (former Chief of Staff to President Clinton) to Kosovo to help government leaders develop improved communication capacity, engage the public in Constitutional processes and develop a homegrown donor strategy.

■ **Moving Forward on Northern Kosovo** *(Washington, DC, 2011/ Medford, MA, 2012)* Organized two expert workshops to evaluate the various current proposals for the North, to develop policy recommendations for a more inclusive negotiation and implementation process, and to consider successful regional models for resolving similar challenges.

BOSNIA AND HERZEGOVINA 1996–1999

After the Dayton Peace Accords were signed in 1995, Richard Holbrooke, the chief architect of the Accords, and United Nations Special Envoy Cyrus Vance asked the Project to help Bosnians from all three communities work toward reconciliation and address the painful, unresolved legacy of missing persons from the war. Key leaders the Project brought to Bosnia and Herzegovina to share their experience included: Salvador Sanabria, FMLN leader from El Salvador; Naomi Chazan, deputy speaker of the Israeli Knesset; Zahira Kamal, general director of gender planning for the Palestinian Authority; Bakhtiar Amin, director of the Human Rights Alliance in Kurdistan; Mbuyi Mhlauli, one of the first to testify in front of South Africa's Truth and Reconciliation Commission; Calixto Torres Santay, a Mayan human rights activist from Guatemala; Joaquín Villalobos, FMLN leader from El Salvador; Monica McWilliams, founder of the Northern Ireland Women's Coalition; and Alex Boraine, former deputy chair of the South African Truth and Reconciliation Commission.

ACCOMPLISHMENTS

■ Played a key role in promoting and beginning a conversation on peace, reconciliation and transitional justice in Bosnia and Herzegovina.

LEFT: General Jovan Divjak and leaders of the Republika Srpska at "Workshop on Reconciliation for Bosnia," London, England, 1996. RIGHT: General Jovan Divjak of Bosnian Army; Salvador Sanabria, representative of the Farabundo Marti National Liberation Front (FMLN) of El Salvador; and Zahira Kamal, Ministry of Planning and International Cooperation, Palestinian Authority, at "The Dynamics of Building Trust: Workshops to Strengthen Dialogue in Bosnia," Sarajevo, 1997.

"After I talked about how hard the process of reconciliation was and how hard it is to understand what happened with the victims, the people from Bosnia asked me, 'How can you solve the problem of your feelings after you know both sides and young people had been killers?' I remember, for ten seconds—a long time—we said nothing. But the only way forward is to think of the future and the young people."

—Joaquín Villalobos, former FMLN Guerilla leader in El Salvador

INITIATIVES

■ **Workshop on Reconciliation for Bosnia** *(London, England, 1996)* Exposed key Bosnians, Croats and Serbs to relevant experiences of international leaders in the aftermath of a violent civil conflict.

■ **The Dynamics of Building Trust: Workshops to Strengthen Dialogue in Bosnia** *(Bosnia, 1997)* Facilitated dialogue on post-conflict reconciliation among Bosnians, Croats and Serbs in Sarajevo, Mostar, Tuzla and Banja Luka.

■ **Conference on Missing Persons for Family Members in the Former Yugoslavia** (Budapest, Hungary, 1997) A forum to examine emotional and practical dimensions of "missing persons" in the former Yugoslavia, Chile, Guatemala, Kurdistan and South Africa.

■ **Bosnian Reconciliation Initiative** *(Budapest, Hungary, 1998)* Enabled discussion among a diverse group from the Bosnian Federation and the Republika Srpska about a range of subjects including concrete measures for in-country follow-up programming.

■ **Strengthening the Role of Women in Politics** *(Zenica, Bosnia, 1999)* Strategic planning on how women can enhance their position in politics and effectively lead a diverse polity.

ABOVE, LEFT: "Workshop on Reconciliation for Bosnia," London, England, 1996. MIDDLE: International participants at "The Dynamics of Building Trust: Workshops to Strengthen Dialogue in Bosnia," Sarajevo, 1997. RIGHT: Dragan Kalinić, Bojislav Valsinovic and Slobodan Kovač at "Workshop on Reconciliation for Bosnia," London, England, 1996. BOTTOM: Mostar, Bosnia.

NORTHERN IRELAND 1994–2004

The Project began working in Northern Ireland in 1994, when it partnered with the University of Ulster to organize a historic gathering of Northern Ireland leaders from across the political spectrum to explore the possibility of peace and reconciliation with leaders who ended Apartheid in South Africa; negotiated the end to a brutal civil war in El Salvador; and worked to build new democratic institutions and confront the legacy of decades of repression in Eastern and Central Europe. It also provided the occasion for the first public meeting of Sinn Fein leaders Gerry Adams and Martin McGuinness with Michael Ancram, the highest ranking British official responsible for peace negotiations, which helped lay the groundwork for the Good Friday Accords. In the following years, the Project organized 17 programs that helped Northern Ireland leaders to develop the skills needed to negotiate a political settlement, develop a shared vision for the future, work toward lasting reconciliation and address the critical issue of demobilization of former combatants. The Project brought over 30 leaders from around the world to Northern Ireland, including: Roelf Meyer, Cyril Ramaphosa, Naomi Chazan, Oscar Arias, Jamil Mahuad, Branka Kaselj, Hasan Abdel Rahman, Antonio Navarro Wolff, Ana Guadalupe Martínez, Hannah Suchocka, Edward M. Kennedy, Jan Urban and Harvard expert on leadership Marty Linsky.

Gerry Adams and Martin McGuinness at "Reconciliation and Community: The Future of Peace in Northern Ireland," Belfast, Northern Ireland, 1995.

ACCOMPLISHMENTS

■ Convened the first public gathering of senior political, governmental and community leaders in Northern Ireland to consider the possibility of peace. That unprecedented meeting and the subsequent 17 initiatives are credited by many leaders in Northern Ireland with playing an instrumental role in their peace process.

■ Assisted party leaders in breaking down barriers between them and developing strong working relationships with each other.

■ Helped the DUP leadership prepare for joint governance with Sinn Fein in the Northern Ireland Assembly.

NORTHERN IRELAND

"Seeing the ways in which other countries had gone that extra mile to resolve intractable conflicts added to our own commitment to make things work"

—Monica McWilliams, Founder of the Northern Ireland Women's Coalition and former member of the Northern Ireland Assembly

LEFT: Lord Alderdice, Mark Durkan and Gerry Adams at "Reconciliation and Community: The Future of Peace in Northern Ireland," Belfast, Northern Ireland, 1995. RIGHT: Nigel Dodds and Peter Robinson at "Session for the Ulster Democratic Unionist Party," Cambridge, Massachusetts, 2004.

INITIATIVES

■ **Reconciliation and Community: The Future of Peace in Northern Ireland** *(Belfast, Northern Ireland, 1995)* Examined Northern Ireland's unfolding transition in light of global experiences in overcoming legacies of conflict.

■ **Managing Change in a Diverse Society** *(Cambridge, Massachusetts, 1996)* Brought together political leaders from Northern Ireland, the Republic of Ireland and Great Britain to consider methods to protect diverse communities and create social cohesion.

■ **Communities Facing Times of Change: Their Role in the Peace-Building Process** *(Belfast, Northern Ireland, 1998)* Allowed a diverse group of over 170 community leaders in Northern Ireland to discuss and analyze the fears, hopes and multi-faceted challenges related to peace-building.

■ **The New Political Architecture** *(Cambridge, Massachusetts, 1998)* Brought together senior leaders from Northern Ireland, the Republic of Ireland and Great Britain to address difficult and pressing issues related to implementing the new peace agreement such as parades, policing and prisoners.

■ **Workshops for Community Leaders in Northern Ireland** *(Northern Ireland, 1998)* Focused on issues related to women, youth, prisoners and victims, as well as on ways in which community groups can have an impact on the peace process in Northern Ireland.

"The most striking moment of that conference was the sense that
those people who had lived a life similar to mine, previously countenancing
violence, had gone through the same process as me: self analysis,
the recognition of the need for change within their society. But I've
also heard of people from South Africa of different colors and it was . . .
absolutely evident, that what divided them was much more than what
divides me from my nationalist neighbor, my catholic neighbor."

—David Ervine, Senior Negotiator in the talks leading to the 1998 Good Friday Agreement
and Chief Spokesman of the Progressive Unionist Party in Northern Ireland.

■ **Remember and Change: Survivors of the Conflict Shaping Their Own Future** *(Templepatrick, Northern Ireland, 1999)* Addressed issues of memory and recognition for a range of individuals and groups who can be considered victims of the Troubles in Northern Ireland.

■ **Community and Governance in a Time of Transition** *(Belfast, Northern Ireland, 1999)* Created a venue for over 200 political and community leaders from throughout Northern Ireland to engage with one another and to discuss priorities and mechanisms for communication and collaboration in the new political environment.

■ **Strategic Perspectives on Governance and Growth** *(Cambridge, Massachusetts, 2001)* Provided executive training for leaders from Northern Ireland, the Republic of Ireland and Great Britain on leadership and management, links between social, political and economic development, and policing.

■ **Rights, Inclusion and Approaches to Dealing with Differences** *(Lusty Beg Island, Northern Ireland, 2001)* Facilitated consideration by 100 community leaders of differences within and between communities, and of the debate surrounding a bill of rights for Northern Ireland.

■ **Crafting Strategies for a Shared Future** *(Belfast, Northern Ireland, 2001)* Created a forum for 150 community and political activists to consider mutually advantageous strategies for action, particularly on the EU's Support Program for Peace and Reconciliation.

■ **Reunion Session for Participants in Executive Training Programs** *(Newcastle, Northern Ireland, 2002)* Through a combination of exercises, case studies and discussions, participants built on their experiences in past programs at the Kennedy School of Government in order to strengthen skills related to leadership and governance.

■ **Extending the Limits: Constraints and Challenges** *(Cambridge, Massachusetts, 2002)* Provided executive training for leaders from Northern Ireland, the Republic of Ireland and Great Britain on leadership and management, participatory planning and alliance building, economic development and rule of law.

LEFT: Hanna Suchocka, MP, Former Prime Minister of Poland; Jerzy Wiatr, MP, Deputy Chairman of the Polish Democratic Left; Joaquín Villalobos, Former Leader of the FMLN Guerrilla Movement; Ambassador Ricardo Castañeda, Permanent Mission of the Republic of El Salvador to the UN; and James LeMoyne, United Nations Political Advisor on the Central American Peace Process, at "Reconciliation and Community: The Future of Peace in Northern Ireland," Belfast, Northern Ireland, 1995. RIGHT: Hasan Abdel Rahman, Chief Representative of the Palestine Liberation Organization to the US; Dullah Omar, Minister of Justice of South Africa; and Arthur Koll, Political Counselor, Embassy of Israel, United Kingdom, at "Reconciliation and Community: The Future of Peace in Northern Ireland," Belfast, Northern Ireland, 1995. BOTTOM: Participants at "Managing Change in a Diverse Society" executive program on Martha's Vineyard, Massachusetts, 1996.

■ **Community Action and Peace-building: Mechanisms for Addressing Difference** *(Belfast, Northern Ireland, 2002)* Allowed 100 community leaders to consider strategies for effective community action in relation to such subjects as young people, victims, human rights, cross-border cooperation, single identity work and peace-building in areas of tension.

■ **Workshop on Strategies for Building Trust in Northern Ireland** *(Cambridge, Massachusetts, 2003)* Designed for 18 leaders to tackle the issue of lack of trust in Northern Ireland – between Catholics and Protestants and between the community and political sectors.

■ **Seminars on Social Action and Peace-Building** *(Northern Ireland, 2003)* In four separate sessions in different parts of Northern Ireland, small groups of community leaders discussed the challenges they face and shared successful strategies they used to address them.

■ **Approaches for Optimizing Opportunities** *(Cambridge, Massachusetts, 2003)* Provided executive training for leaders from Northern Ireland, the Republic of Ireland and Great Britain on campaign strategies, persuasion, leadership and participatory planning.

■ **Working Together for Sustainable Peace** (Templepatrick, Northern Ireland, 2003) Presentations by practitioners from Northern Ireland and elsewhere, along with working groups, allowed over 100 participants to examine the challenges for community and political action in Northern Ireland.

■ **Session for the Ulster Democratic Unionist Party** *(Cambridge, Massachusetts, 2004)* A session for senior members of the Democratic Unionist Party that examined strategies related to governance, negotiation and persuasion, leadership and risk-taking.

LATIN AMERICA
1992–2012

LATIN AMERICA

The Project on Justice in Times of Transition has been working with Latin American leaders since its inaugural conference in Salzburg, Austria, in 1992. The Project was invited to assist leaders in El Salvador consider paths to reconciliation following the signing of the 1992 Chapultepec Peace Accords; to address reconciliation and lingering tensions in Nicaragua after the 1990 elections that brought Violeta Chamorro to power; and to work toward strengthening peace in Guatemala following the 1996 peace agreement between the government and the URNG guerrilla movement. The Project also worked in Peru and Guatemala to strengthen democratic oversight of intelligence services, helped the government of Colombia and the ELN guerilla movement prepare for negotiations and exposed the latter to experiences from elsewhere concerning reintegrating former combatants. The Project brought key leaders to the region from Northern Ireland, South Africa, Eastern Europe and the Middle East, including: Lech Wałęsa, former leader of Solidarity and the first post-communist president of Poland; General Wojciech Jaruzelski, president of Poland under martial law; David Ervine, a former paramilitary and leader of the Progressive Unionist Party in Northern Ireland; Jan Urban, Czech former dissident; Adam Michnik, former dissident and editor of *Gazeta Wyborcza* in Poland; and former US President Jimmy Carter.

ACCOMPLISHMENTS

■ Played a key role in promoting negotiations towards peace, reconciliation and transitional justice in El Salvador, Nicaragua, Colombia and Guatemala.

"My first encounter with the Project on Justice in Times of Transition was in 1993 in San Salvador, soon after the signing of our peace accords, for the event, 'Reconciliation in Times of Transition.' For the first time officers of the Salvadoran army were sharing the same roof with me, a recently demobilized ex-guerrilla. . . . These experiences mean discoveries and comparisons between the experience of one group and that of the other. The result is a communication between people of very different positions that sensitizes, enriches knowledge and understanding and diminishes mistrust. This is an important step in achieving the long-term objective of justice and peace."

— ANA GUADALUPE MARTINEZ, HEAD OF THE SENATE IN EL SALVADOR AND FORMER FMLN GUERILLA LEADER

INITIATIVES

■ **Reconciliation in Times of Transition** *(San Salvador, El Salvador, 1993)* Focused on consolidating peace and eradicating social division, confrontation and political violence in the aftermath of El Salvador's peace accords. Precipitated the creation of Centro Demos, the conflict resolution center established to encourage and sustain cross-sectoral dialogue.

■ **Reflections on Transition** *(Managua, Nicaragua, 1994)* Brought together prominent Nicaraguan leaders with their counterparts from Europe and the Americas to discuss reconciliation, civil-military relations, private property and economic reform.

OPPOSITE, LEFT: President Lech Wałęsa of Poland with Leonel Gomez of El Salvador during "The Challenge of Strengthening the Peace," Guatemala City, Guatemala, 1999. OPPOSITE, RIGHT: Paul Arthur of Northern Ireland speaking at "The Challenge of Strengthening the Peace," Guatemala City, Guatemala, 1999. ABOVE, LEFT: James LeMoyne, UN Political Advisor to Central America; Joaquín Villalobos, Farabundo Marti National Liberation Front; and Adam Michnik, Editor-in-Chief, *Gazeta Wyborzca*, during "Reflections on Transition," Managua, Nicaragua, 1994. ABOVE, RIGHT: Manuel Conde Orellana, former President of the Guatemalan Commission for Peace; Augusto Ramírez Ocampo, former Foreign Minister of Colombia and former Special Representative of the UN Secretary-General to El Salvador; Vinicio Cerezo, former President of Guatemala; Oscar Santamaría, former head negotiator for El Salvador; and Rodrigo Madrigal Nieto, former Foreign Minister of Costa Rica, during "Lessons Learned on Regional Peace-building in Central America," Toledo, Spain, 2006.

LEFT: Joaquín Villalobos, Former Leader of the FMLN Guerilla Movement during "Reconciliation in Times of Transition," San Salvador, El Salvador, 1993. RIGHT: Participants at "Reconciliation in Times of Transition," San Salvador, El Salvador, 1993, including Héctor Gramajo, Roberto Cañas, Antonio Navarro Wolff, Jim McGovern, Zbigniew Bujak, Jan Urban, Aleksander Kwaśniewski, Stephen Heintz, George Biddle, Ambler Moss, Joe Montville and Rafael Nunez among others. OPPOSITE: Father Alec Reid, intermediary and peace faciliator, Northern Ireland; David Ervine, Chief Spokesman, Progressive Unionist Party, Northern Ireland; Tom Roberts, Director, Ex Prisoners' Interpretive Center, Northern Ireland; Francisco Galán, ELN Commissioner, Colombia; and Wendy Luers, Project Co-Founder, during "Negotiating from Conflict to Peace: Workshop with the Colombian ELN," Medellin, Colombia, 2006.

■ **The Challenge of Strengthening the Peace** *(Guatemala City, Guatemala, 1999)* Brought together over 300 Guatemalan representatives of the government, the military, the church, political parties, the private sector, human rights organizations and community groups to engage in dialogue on a range of issues critical to peace-building in their country.

■ **Reform of Intelligence and Security Services in Guatemala** *(Cambridge, Massachusetts, 2000)* Brought together senior members of the new Guatemalan government with intelligence officials from the Americas, Africa and Europe to discuss key issues related to reforming and restructuring the Guatemalan intelligence apparatus.

■ **International Perspectives on Intelligence Reform and Creating Democratic Controls** *(Guatemala City, Guatemala, 2000)* Enabled Guatemalan government officials, members of NGOs and academics to meet with intelligence experts from around the world in order to discuss experiences of reform, outline mechanisms of oversight and gain feedback on recommendations for a new intelligence law in Guatemala.

■ **Combating Terrorism: The Challenge for Democratic Societies** *(Cambridge, Massachusetts, 2002)* Leaders from the intelligence and law enforcement communities in Mexico, Peru and the United States discussed strategies for combating terrorism while protecting human rights and democratic freedoms.

■ **Peruvian Intelligence Reform Initiative** *(Cambridge, Massachusetts, and Lima, Peru, 2002)* Convened international experts on internal security to draft recommendations for reforming Peru's intelligence services and presented the results to the Peruvian intelligence community in a public forum event in Lima.

■ **Lessons Learned on Regional Peace-building in Central America** *(Toledo, Spain, 2006)* Brought together all major leaders involved in developing the regional peace accords in Central America to launch a task force that will develop new approaches to rule of law challenges faced in the region today.

"What impressed the ELN negotiating team was how the Project was able to come up with a group of people from all over the world within two weeks and was able to create a unique kind of space where different and new kinds of solutions and possibilities of peace could be imagined. At the same time, the people they brought made a space where motivation and aspiration was created. That was a very important, concrete contribution."

—Aldo Civico, Director, International Institute for Peace, Rutgers University

■ **La Nicaragua Possible** *(Managua, Nicaragua, 2006)* Brought together leading Nicaraguan politicians, intellectuals and students to discuss the challenges facing the country and strategize future solutions.

■ **Negotiating from Conflict to Peace: Workshop with the Colombian ELN** *(Medellin, Colombia, 2006)* Workshop that brought three senior leaders from Northern Ireland and the Republic of Ireland to share experiences in managing the transition from paramilitary organization to political leadership.

■ **The Challenge of Verification in Peace Processes** *(Bogotá and Medellin, Colombia, 2007)* Conducted workshops sharing comparative experiences on arms verification and ceasefire management for the Colombian government and the ELN guerilla group.

■ **Politics without Violence** *(Bogotá, Colombia, 2008)* Created several fora for members of the Colombian Senate and civil society to discuss current obstacles to a peace process and how to reframe and legitimize the government/ELN dialogue.

■ **Leaders of the Present: Youth Leadership and Civic Engagement in Central America** *(Antigua, Guatemala, 2008)* A five day meeting with 24 young Central American leaders to facilitate development of action plans on youth engagement on regional issues such as youth violence and disaster risk reduction (especially in relation to climate change).

■ **Reconciliation and Change** *(Miami, 2012)* A one day meeting that brought together over 80 Cuban American leaders to consider how reconciliation and change was generated in South Africa and Northern Ireland—part of an effort to help Cuban Americans better understand their role in improving US/Cuban relations.

SOUTH AFRICA

SOUTH AFRICA 1994

Following a meeting with Nelson Mandela during his visit to the United States in 1993, the Project was invited to help the new South African leadership with the tasks of strengthening democracy and promoting reconciliation in the aftermath of Apartheid. In 1994, the Project partnered with the Institute for a Democratic Alternative for South Africa (IDASA) to organize a historic conference in Somerset West that brought leaders from Latin America and Central and Eastern Europe to share their experiences in confronting the legacies of dictatorship and past human rights abuses with South African leaders who were considering how best to tackle the painful legacies of Apartheid. Participants from South Africa and elsewhere included: Richard Goldstone, Albie Sachs, Dullah Omar, Alex Boraine, Mary Burton, Adam Michnik, José Zalaquett, Joachim Gauck, Karel Schwarzenberg, Patricio Aylwin, András Sajó, Lawrence Weschler and Tina Rosenberg.

ACCOMPLISHMENTS

■ Introduced the idea of a truth commission to South Africa as the principal vehicle for dealing with its past during a historic meeting in Cape Town in 1994.

INITIATIVES

■ **Dealing with the Past** *(Cape Town, South Africa, 1994)* Focused on confronting the legacies of prior repression, building democracy and fostering post-Apartheid national reconciliation. Discussions at this meeting contributed to the subsequent creation of the South African Truth and Reconciliation Commission.

"It was a watershed time for South Africa, the question of a TRC [Truth and Reconciliation Commission] was very much up in the air....it was at that time that the Project held this meeting on transitional justice, and that certainly played a role in convincing opinion leaders that a TRC was important. . . ."

—RICHARD GOLDSTONE, FORMER HEAD OF THE GOLDSTONE COMMISSION

SRI LANKA
2002

At the invitation of Prime Minister Ranil Wickramasinghe and Sri Lankan Senior Government Peace Negotiator Melinda Maragoda, the Project assisted the government of Sri Lanka and the Liberation Tigers of Tamil Eeelam (LTTE) prepare for peace negotiations. The Project brought leaders from Latin America and South Africa to work with both parties, and the South Africans continue to play an active role in assisting Sri Lanka's leaders.

ACCOMPLISHMENTS

■ Played a key role in promoting negotiations towards peace, reconciliation and transitional justice in Sri Lanka.

TOP: José María Argueta and Milinda Moragoda, Government Negotiator, during "Preparing for Negotiations," Colombo, Sri Lanka, 2002. BOTTOM: William Weisberg, Columbia University; Joaquín Villalobos, former FMLN Commander; Donna Hicks, Harvard University; David Ervine, head of the PUP in Northern Ireland; José María Argueta, former Guatemalan ambassador to Japan; and Tim Phillips, Project Chair, at "Preparing for Negotiations," Colombo, Sri Lanka, 2002.

INITIATIVES

■ **Preparing for Negotiations** *(Colombo, Sri Lanka, 2002)* Held a small consultation for key members of the Sri Lankan government preparing for their first round of discussions with senior representatives of the Liberation Tigers of Tamil Eelam (LTTE) during the summer of 2002.

"What was most compelling about bringing David Ervine, José María Argueta and Joaquín Villalobos with us to Sri Lanka was the respect they commanded from the top officials with whom we met. Having gone through all the difficult and often painful steps to achieving peace, our team was able to provide insight and vision for the Sri Lankans when they needed it the most. In addition to providing a sense of hope and possibility, David, José María, and Joaquín offered a big dose of compassion for what the Sri Lankan's were going through. It was fascinating seeing them in action."

—DONNA HICKS, WEATHERHEAD CENTER FOR INTERNATIONAL AFFAIRS, HARVARD UNIVERSITY

THE MIDDLE EAST
AND NORTH AFRICA
1999–2013

In 2000, Palestinian National Authority President Yasser Arafat invited the Project to help Palestinians prepare for statehood and to train senior government officials in democratic governance and leadership. The Project worked with the John F. Kennedy School of Government at Harvard University to facilitate lessons learned from several transitional societies. In 2006, the Project partnered with Tufts University to launch the Iraq Moving Forward Initiative, which resulted in the Helsinki Accords on peace and reconciliation. More recently, in response to the Arab Spring, the Project has been working in Bahrain to help create a space for dialogue between the government and the Shia and Sunni opposition. Prominent leaders from other countries that the Project has brought to the region include: David Trimble, former first minister of Northern Ireland; José María Argueta, Guatemala's first civilian national security advisor; Albie Sachs, former dissident and member of the Constitutional Court of South Africa; Mohammed Bhabha, legal advisor to the constitutional committee of South Africa's African National Congress; Ebrahim Ebrahim, deputy foreign minister of South Africa; Maria Eugenia Brizuela de Avila, foreign minister of El Salvador; Paul Arthur of University of Ulster in Northern Ireland; and Ana Guadalupe Martínez, former FMLN leader in El Salvador.

ACCOMPLISHMENTS

■ Helped prepare Bahraini leaders for eventual dialogue by sharing experiences and thereby broadening perspectives and helping to identify local solutions.

LEFT: Albie Sachs, former Justice, South African Constitutional Court; Yasser Arafat, President of the Palestinian National Authority; and Jerzy Osiatyński, member of the Polish Parliament, former Minister of Finance, at "Fortifying the Foundations of a Nation: Strengthening Governance in the Palestinian National Authority," Gaza, 2000. RIGHT: Mac Maharaj, Former ANC Negotiator in talks with the National Party Government, South Africa, and Ali Allawi, Former Minister of Defense and Minister of Trade, Interim Iraq Government Council, Former Minister of Finance, Iraqi Transitional Government, at "Iraq Moving Forward," Boston, 2007.

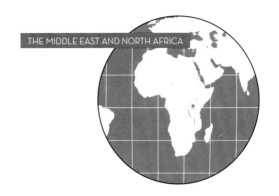

"As someone who has been actively involved in the MENA region for over twenty years, I have been particularly struck by the power and role that the Project can play in helping countries and leaders involved in transition understand and overcome conflict. In Bahrain, the Project has managed to develop and deploy a unique methodology of shared experience that addresses not just the political, historical and economic drivers and consequences of conflict but also the psychological and personal ones as well."

—MARK MULLER, QC, DIRECTOR, BEYOND BORDERS

INITIATIVES

■ **Fortifying the Foundations of a Nation: Strengthening Governance in the Palestinian National Authority** *(Gaza, 2000)* Convened a meeting for over 300 Palestinian government officials, civil servants, community actors, business-people and academics on the challenges of governance and institution-building in the Palestinian National Authority.

■ **Iraq Moving Forward** *(Boston, 2007)* Brought together several key Iraqi officials with leading international players from divided societies in order to share lessons learned and consider steps for reconciliation and an end to violence in Iraq.

■ **Creating a Roadmap for Bahrain** *(Manama, Bahrain: June 2011, October 2011, Feb. 2012, Nov. 2012, Feb. 2013)* A quiet effort designed to help create a space for meaningful dialogue between the opposition and the government of Bahrain.

ABOVE: Roelf Meyer, former Chief Negotiator for F.W. de Klerk in South Africa; Abdulaziz Hassan Ali Abula, Shura Council member; Esam Abdulla Fakhro, Chamber of Industry and Commerce; and Mohammed Bhabba, ANC activist and negotiator to the Constitution, during "Creating a Roadmap for Bahrain," Manama, 2011.

UNITED NATIONS AND RULE OF LAW 2002–2007

In 2002, the United Nations invited the Project to help it assess the impact of UN peacekeeping operations and to assess whether UN efforts to promote the rule of law were successful. The Project brought local leaders from East Timor, Bosnia and Herzegovina, Kosovo, Cambodia, Afghanistan and other countries where the United Nations had established major missions in the recent past to share their experiences directly with the highest levels of the United Nations through its partners, which included the United Nations Association and the Task Force for the Development of Comprehensive Rule of Law Strategies for Peace Operations (led by the Department of Peacekeeping Operations). The resulting recommendations fed into the Brahimi Report process and the eventual establishment of the United Nations Peacebuilding Commission and Peacebuilding Support Office. Prominent international participants and United Nations representatives in our programs included: Under-Secretary-General of the Department of Peacekeeping Operations Jean-Marie Guéhenno; Under-Secretary-General for Legal Affairs Hans Corell; Mark Malloch Brown, head of the United Nations Development Programme; Ambassador of Singapore to the UN Kishore Mahbubani; Ambassador of Jordan to the UN Prince Zeid Ra'ad Zeid Al-Hussein; former Foreign Minister of Australia Gareth Evans; and President of Botswana Ketumile Masire.

ACCOMPLISHMENTS

■ Successfully helped the UN introduce recommendations on how to improve rule of law practice and implementation during field operations on the ground.

LEFT: Ian Martin, former Special Representative to the Secretary-General of the UN to East Timor, and Wendy Luers, Project Co-Founder, at "Incorporating Local Voices into International Rule of Law Strategies," Singapore, 2001. RIGHT: Jacinta Correia da Costa, Judge, District Court, Dili, East Timor, and Gareth Evans, President of the International Crisis Group and former Foreign Minister of Australia, at "Incorporating Local Voices into International Rule of Law Strategies," Singapore, 2001.

LEFT: Behrooz Sadry, Deputy Special Representative of the Secretary-General for Sierra Leone, UNMSL, at "Establishing Rule of Law and Governance in Post Conflict Societies," Istanbul, Turkey, 2002. RIGHT: Robert Rotberg, World Peace Foundation, and Tim Phillips at "The Experience of Local Actors in Peacebuilding, Reconstruction and the Establishment of Rule of Law," Istanbul, Turkey 2002.

"The primary responsibility for developing a comprehensive rule of law strategy for a country emerging from conflict and for its long-term implementation should ultimately rest with the people of the country concerned. The Project/UNA initiative was designed to help us do this better in the future."

—JEAN MARIE GUÉHENNO, FORMER UNDER-SECRETARY-GENERAL, DEPARTMENT OF PEACEKEEPING OPERATIONS, UNITED NATIONS

INITIATIVES

■ **The Experience of Local Actors in Peacebuilding, Reconstruction and the Establishment of Rule of Law** *(Singapore, 2002)* Gathered local leaders, lawyers, civil society practitioners and UN officials from Cambodia, East Timor and Kosovo to share experiences on UN peacebuilding efforts in their country.

■ **Establishing Rule of Law and Governance in Post Conflict Societies** *(Istanbul, Turkey, 2002)* Enabled 40 practitioners from Afghanistan, Bosnia, Cambodia, East Timor, El Salvador, Kosovo and Sierra Leone to draft recommendations on efforts to establish rule of law in the context of UN peace operations

■ **Incorporating Local Voices into International Rule of Law Strategies: A Policy Dialogue** *(New York, 2002)* Brought a group of national leaders and practitioners from Cambodia, East Timor, El Salvador, Haiti, Kosovo and Bosnia and Herzegovina to New York to share their views on UN peace-building with senior decision-makers at the United Nations

■ **Rule of Law and the Legacy of Conflict** *(Gaborone, Botswana, 2003)* Assembled over 40 practitioners from 10 African states (including Angola, Congo, Nigeria and Sierra Leone) and 8 other countries to discuss and develop recommendations for improving rule of law efforts in United Nations peacebuilding operations.

■ **Rule of Law and the United Nations: The Critical Path to Post-Conflict Justice** *(New York, 2003)* Presented the comprehensive list of recommendations developed in Singapore, Istanbul and Gabarone to high-level officials at the UN and key member state representatives.

■ **Broadening the UN's Access to Qualified Candidates for the Field** *(New York, 2007)* Brought together high-level UN policy makers and leading member state roster representatives to discuss DPKO needs with regard to civilian staffing for future peacekeeping operations.

NEUROSCIENCE
AND SOCIAL CONFLICT
2012–present

In 2012, the Project launched a groundbreaking initiative in partnership with the SaxeLab at MIT that explores how the new tools of neuroscience can help us better understand the relationships between the brain, violence and universal human reactions to conflict. Discovering how the brain processes the experience of conflict will allow us to decipher some of the mechanisms that contribute to violence and influence the decision-making capacity of citizens, negotiators and leaders in societies engaged in conflict. The program's first two meetings brought together cognitive neuroscientists, social psychologists, political scientists, experienced leaders from societies affected by conflict and conflict management experts, including: Elizabeth Phelps, Rebecca Saxe, Emile Bruneau, Mohammed Milad, Susan Fiske, Nick Hanson, Lee Ross, Herbert Kelman, Dan Batson, Gary Slutkin, Donna Hicks, Eileen Babbitt, Jamil Mahuad, José María Argueta, Paul Arthur, Jan Urban, Roger Peterson, Paul Zak, Jamil Zaki and many others.

ACCOMPLISHMENTS

■ Launched a groundbreaking initiative to bring together leading scientists and practitioners to learn how neuroscience can help us better understand human conflict and improve conflict resolution and public diplomacy strategies globally. The multi-year initiative will convene leading scientists to undertake new research and engage practitioners to help translate these findings to key audiences.

LEFT: Rebecca Saxe, head of the SaxeLab, MIT. MIDDLE: Mohammed Bhabha, member of the ANC legal negotiating team. RIGHT: Jessica Stern, author and Project Board member. OPPOSITE: Roelf Meyer, former Chief Negotiator for F.W. de Klerk. Participants at "Neuroscience and Social Conflict," Cambridge, Massachusetts, 2012.

"The collaboration with the Project is unique in that it offers us (neuroscientists) access to people who have a deep, personal understanding of intergroup conflict —this both informs our intuitions about what to study and how, and gives us the opportunity to examine how the brain processes conflict in real-world situations. This has facilitated a unique interdisciplinary conversation that is nurturing a new generation of scientists to look at conflict resolution and help develop tools to better evaluate existing practices."

— Emile Bruneau, SaxLab, MIT

BOARDS AND COMMITTEES

ACKNOWLEDGMENTS

There are many amazing and generous people who have given their time, resources and wisdom to make the Project on Justice in Times of Transition possible. Most important among them are Wendy Luers, Project Co-Founder, who recognized the opportunity of the idea and has nurtured the Project to this day; Tim Phillips, Project Chair, whose inspired idea that people can learn from the experience of others and whose creativity, passion and vision guide the organization to this day; and Ina Breuer, who has served as Executive Director of the Project for more than eight years and whose dedication, leadership and hard work have allowed the Project to thrive over the past decade. There are also many staff members who contributed their devotion and energy over the years, including: Mary Albon, Eric Nonacs, Sonja Valtasaari, Sara Zucker, Andrea Boldt, Eva Canoutas, Jenny Ellis, Stan Byers, Mauricio Artinano, Adam Levy, Kevin Martin, Kelsi Stine, Ben Harburg, Alex Busse, Ariel Berney and Lee-Or Ankori-Karlinsky.

The Project has benefited from the expertise and passion of many individuals who have helped shape the content of its work and design its initiatives. These include: Tim Ryback, Sherman Teichman, Lloyd Cutler, Herman Schwartz, Ruti Teitel, Diane Orentlicher, Herb Gleason, Roger Lort, Lawrence Weschler, Neil Kritz, Tina Rosenberg, Priscilla Hayner, John Tirman, Allan Ryan, Nancy Soderberg, Frank Loy, Robert Hutchings, Deborah Harding, Jan Urban, George Biddle, James LeMoyne, José María Argueta, Jim McGovern, Jim O'Brien, Saul Suster, Dick McCall, Carolyn Forche, Tara Magner, Wade Green, Adrian Basora, Jim Hoge, Harry Barnes, President William Jefferson Clinton, President Jimmy Carter, President Andres Pastrana, Prime Minister Felipe Gonzalez, Ivor Jenkins, Mohammed Bhabha, Hasan Abdel Rahman, Gutavo Porras, Pierre Schori, Harvey Fineberg, Rose Styron, Olin Robinson, Arturo Cruz Jr, Leonel Gomez, Antonio Lacayo, Tim Reiser, John Maisto, Kent Shreve, Alex Boraine, Sir John Birch, John Healy, Paul Arthur, Avila Kilmurray, Jean Kennedy Smith, Stephen Smith, Senator Edward M. Kennedy, Phillip Heymann, Peter Zimmerman, Jim Cooney, Nina Lahoud, David Scheffer, William Luers, Herb Kelman, Antonia Chayes, Steve Reifenberg, Samantha Power, Anne-Marie Slaughter, Robert Rotberg, Donna Hicks, Brian Mandell, Prime Minister Kim Campbell, Diego Hildago, Sanna Johnson, Bill Walker, Fron Nahzi, Stephen Heintz, Madeleine Albright, Frank Wisner, Haki Abazi, Aldo Civico, Ram Manikkalingam, Eileen Babbitt, Mari Fitzduff, Bruce Hitchner, Roelf Meyer, Mohammed Bhabha, Mark Muller QC, Sean Carroll, Emile Bruneau, Rebecca Saxe, David Taffel, Ted Piconne, Carlos Saladrigas, Hugh O'Doherty and Dean Williams.

In addition, there are many generous funders who supported the Project over the years and recognized the value of shared experience in the service of peace and reconciliation. In particular the Project on Justice in Times of Transition would like to thank George Soros and the Open Society Institute for supporting its work from the very beginning, along with Atlantic Philanthropies, the Hewlett Foundation and Frank Giustra who have been key funders throughout the years. The Project has also received support from the Middle East Partnership Initiative of the US Department of State, the Radcliffe

Foundation, the Winston Foundation, the Rockefeller Brothers Fund, the Rockefeller Foundation, Rockefeller Family and Associates, the Carnegie Corporation of New York, the German Marshall Fund of the United States, Charles Stewart Mott Foundation, Christopher Reynolds Foundation, Olof Palme International Center, the British Foreign Commonwealth Office, the US State Department, the United Nations Foundation, the American Ireland Fund, the Compton Foundation, the Ford Foundation, FRIDE, the German Ministry of Foreign Affairs, Cisneros Group, Harvard Law School, Joyce Mertz-Gilmore Foundation, the National Endowment for Democracy, the Toledo Center for International Peace, US Agency for International Development, United Nations Development Program, the David Rockefeller Center for Latin American Studies at Harvard University, the Kunstadter Family Foundation, the Luce Foundation, Mutual Life of America, the National Democratic Institute, the US AID Office of Transition Initiatives, the Organization for Security and Co-operation in Europe Mission in Kosovo, the Tinker Foundation, the Woods Foundation, the Club of Madrid, ASI Investments, DLA Piper, the Eurasia Foundation, the European Commission, the Government of Colombia, the Howard Gilman Foundation, the Inter-American Development Bank, John Cullinane, the Joseph Rowntree Charitable Trust, National University of Singapore, the Slifka Foundation, the Hauser Foundation, INCORE, J.M. Kaplan Fund, the Park Foundation, the Samuel Rubin Foundation, Carolyn Seeley Wiener, Bernard Aidinoff, Nancy Rubin, Paul and Catherine Buttenwieser, Amed Khan, Yousef Abbas, Phil Villers, Jack Levin, Kim Brizzolara, Maurice Templesman, Renata Schwebel, Rona Kiley, Warren and Meagan Adams and Ben Heineman.

In the course of our twenty-year history, the Project on Justice in Times of Transition has had a number of very supportive institutional homes and partners, beginning with the Foundation for a Civil Society in New York (formerly the Charter 77 Foundation-New York). From the Project's inception, the Foundation for a Civil Society nurtured it and stepped in at key moments to help it develop and grow. From 1999 to 2004 the Project on Justice in Times of Transition was based at Harvard University as a university-wide initiative affiliated with Harvard Law School, the Weatherhead Center for International Affairs and the John F. Kennedy School of Government and thanks Phil Heymann for that incredible opportunity and wonderful partnership. The Project was also lucky, thanks to the remarkable Sherman Teichman, to have a close, intellectually vibrant and enormously supportive strategic partnership with the Institute for Global Leadership (IGL) at Tufts University from 2006 to 2013.

Finally, a special thanks to those who helped write and assemble this book: Mary Albon, Tim Phillips, Ariel Berney, Kelsi Stine, Lee-Or Ankori-Karlinsky, Emily Clayton, David Taffel, Ina Breuer, Mary Daly, Yolanda Cuomo, Kristi Norgaard and Bonnie Briant. Three amazing photographers also contributed to the book: Elizabeth Herman, Anna Schori and Ramsay Turnbull.

For more information on the Project on Justice in Times of Transition see www.pjtt.org or www.beyondconflictint.org

BEYOND CONFLICT

THE PROJECT ON JUSTICE IN TIMES OF TRANSITION

20 YEARS OF PUTTING EXPERIENCE TO WORK FOR PEACE

All photographs © The Project on Justice in Times of Transition except for the following images:

Pages 8, 29, 32, 39, 42, 49, 52, 59, and the front cover: © Elizabeth Herman

Page 4: © Paolo Pellegrin/Magnum Photos

Page 6: © Ian Berry/Magnum Photos

Page 12: © Mark Power/Magnum Photos

Page 18: © Xinhua/eyevine/Redux

Page 20: © Ian Berry/Mangnum Photos

Page 23: © Anna Schori

Page 24: © Democracy Digest

Page 30–31: © Ian Berry/Magnum Photos

Page 40–41: © Larry Towell/Magnum Photos

Page 46: © AP Photo/Eugene Hoshiko

Pages 50–51: © Bettmann/CORBIS

Pages 60–61: © Noam Armonn/Spaces Images/Corbis

Page 63: © Paolo Pellegrin/Magnum Photos

Pages 66–67: © Paolo Pellegrin/Magnum Photos

Pages 68–69: © Carlos Carrion/Sygma/Corbis

Pages 71 and 77: © Ramsay Turnbull

Page 82: © Paolo Pellegrin/Magnum Photos

The back cover: © Paolo Pellegrin/Magnum Photos

First Edition 2013

ISBN 978-0-615-79057-2

Book Design by Yolanda Cuomo, NYC
Associate Designer: Kristi Norgaard
Assistant Designer: Bonnie Briant

Printing and binding by EBS Editoriatle Bortolazzi, Verona

Printed and bound in Italy